Jo Herlihy

THE HOUSE of PUBLISHING

Alchemy: A Search for Truth

By Jo Herlihy

Publisher: The House of Publishing

ISBN 978-1-9162808-0-9 Amazon Kindle

ISBN 978-1-9162808-1-6 Paperback

Cover design by Jan Bowman
Graphics by lastwerd

For Drew…because you can, and you do

CONTENTS

Acknowledgements

A very big thank you to Travis J Dow, co-creator of The History of Alchemy podcast series, for helping me cook up the idea for this book; Esme Gill-Brown for your experiments in design; Jan Bowman for fusing so many images together into a single cover design; and Anna Keenan and Nicky Drury for working your magic through the transmutation of my sentences - however, all mistakes and factual errors, I claim as my own.

Finally a very special thank you to Drew who helped me, and a horse-load of books, make it over the alps.

"Keep far away from impia curiositas...."

Desiderius Erasmus 1518

Introduction

This book was inspired by the fascinating, character-driven, the *History of Alchemy* podcast series[1] created by Travis Dow and Peter Collman[i] and by the annual The Academy event that explores philosophy, history and culture[ii]. The majority of the book covers the one and a half thousand years from when alchemy became a specific practice. It provides a chronological, descriptive narrative of the characters featured in the podcast series and the ideas that surrounded many of those drawn towards alchemy, helping explain what attracted so many to this art.

The book examines how questions people thought reasonable to ask and seek answers to were regarded. It necessarily also looks at why difficult concepts, such as transmutation and change, have been so important in the development of ideas.

What is alchemy?

A helpful definition of alchemy is provided by Adam Mclean, an established authority on alchemical texts and symbolism:

> *"Alchemy is a multifaceted subject. It is an early form of chemical technology exploring the nature of substances. It is also a philosophy of the cosmos and of mankind's place in the*

---

[1] All series episodes referred to in the text are underlined

> *incorporated religious metaphor and spiritual matters into their alchemical ideas."* [iii]

Alchemy began around the 3rd to 4th centuries AD in Roman ruled Egypt, yet it seems older - born from ancient knowledge. The word 'alchemy' is likely have originated from the Arabic interest in this practice around AD 700 but, for simplicity, this term is used throughout this text.

Alchemy did not spring from nowhere. Prior to it becoming a specific practice, there had been centuries of experimentation, trial and error and the development of new forms of technologies as people tried to control and shape the world around them.

Alongside the inventiveness and industriousness of different communities, the unsettling questions of life and death, and the anxiety created by forces beyond one's control, resulted in people delving into the mysteries of life.

These mysteries gave rise to magic, divination and alchemy. People wondered if they could gain immortality and some looked for an *elixir of life* that would give them this. They wondered how life could be bettered and how to get nature to offer up its secrets.

Some thought it would be possible to unlock nature's secret by discovering how the perfection of material substances and objects is achieved. Combining a philosophical outlook with experimental practice, this became the search for how to turn base metals into gold. To make this transmutation possible, a substance, known as the *philosopher's stone*, was needed.

Alchemy incorporates sacred ritual and practical knowledge found in many ancient texts. From its earliest days, alchemy was practised in advanced civilisations and backed by powerful people. It engaged some of the most curious minds searching for fundamental truths about the world.

This study focuses on the practice of alchemy within the civilisations surrounding the Mediterranean including southern and northern Europe, North Africa and some of western Asia. Although a complete history of alchemy would also consider developments within India and China, this study confines itself to a smaller geographical area in order to explore the relationships between alchemy, modern science and Western Religion and Philosophy.

Throughout the recounting of this chronological story, there are three inter-woven topics that help provide a context for understanding alchemy and its appeal to people over many centuries. These topics are the search for Truth, mystery and reason and third, the physical journey and care of knowledge, essential in the search for Truth.

Firstly, on Truth. Describing some of the main ideas of the key periods when alchemy was practised, this book establishes what the broad philosophical and religious ideas were. In each era when alchemy was practised, its focus was weighted towards either the practical side of experimentation or the spiritual aspects of divining Truth. However, for alchemy to be a distinct practice, a relationship between these two sides was needed.

One aim of this book it to gain an understanding of the different world outlooks in each of the different epochs and why some of the most creative minds, regardless of religion, looked to alchemy for answers.

Second, the book explores the concepts of mystery and reason and what the relationship has been between them. I explore whether alchemy was regarded as a mystical practice of magic or one grounded in logic and reason.

There is no doubt that the practical experimentation undertaken by alchemists provided real insights and new knowledge, bringing real benefits to society and also paved the way for modern chemistry. But alchemy is mercurial, usually being practised alongside a panoply of other ideas and where a clear line between mystery and reason could not easily be discerned.

Despite this tension between mystery and reason, grappling with alchemy often proved to be a hugely creative activity. It often required going beyond conventional wisdom and using knowledge that often rested in the hands of kings, priests and philosophers who acted as the gatekeepers of this resource.

However, balanced against the danger of going against the grain was inquisitiveness, curiosity and a self-conscious effort to understand the world. Even if this was a perilous activity and could result in a deadly fate, the desire within people to find their own answers, away from the gaze of the gatekeepers, often compelled people to look beyond orthodoxy.

It is in this space the space between mystery and reason that the human imagination thrived.

Third, this book describes the physical journey and storage of the knowledge that was so essential for the development and practice of alchemy – and for establishing truth. The ideas and knowledge that were developed were revered and sometime, like scripture, treated as sacred. This important status is reflected in the way knowledge was stored and treasured.

Throughout the journey of knowledge, civilisations were continually uprooted and moved on, their texts and mythologies moving with them, or being taken from them. Texts might have been seized as spoils of war, or given as gifts, exchanged between the mighty heads of grand civilisations. Old texts, including those important for the development of alchemy, were carefully transported, sometimes for thousands of miles, and then preserved, treasured and copied down the ages. Priests, princes, philosophers, physicians, emperors, caliphs, mystics and astrologers are amongst those who originated, transcribed, developed and shaped the ideas within these manuscripts.

Introduction

The titles of each of the eight chapters of this book refer to temples, churches, schools, libraries and cities, whether real or utopian, where knowledge was housed. It seems that anchoring knowledge in distinct places, as collections, allowed it to become solid, tethering it in time and space. These important real or conceptual storehouses gave status to knowledge – and to the philosophers, scholars and priests associated with these revered places. Such centres became magnets for those interested in ideas and creativity and, inevitably, the places where alchemists were active, even when their practice was undertaken behind a veil of secrecy.

The inter-twining of alchemy with multiple religious and philosophical ideas had wider significance. This book attempts to describe the evolution of alchemy within the wider development of Western philosophical and religious thinking.

Alchemy and knowledge have often been uncomfortable companions – but mostly it was the possibility of finding an underlying Truth that compelled them on together. Beyond this Truth, many hoped to find meaning.

Note:
'BC' and 'AD' are used throughout as the development of knowledge described in this book takes place in a specific historical context where Christianity provides an overall arc of influence and where time has subsequently been conceived of from this perspective - an important context for the development of alchemy in the West.

Introduction

'Man' is used throughout as it represents the scientific category used to determine what is unique and distinct in our being compared to other species of animal

CHAPTER ONE

THE HOUSE OF LIFE to PLATO'S KALLIPOLIS AND MAGNESIA

WHEN and WHERE

6500 - 322 BC

EGYPT • MESOPOTAMIA • BABYLONIA • GREECE

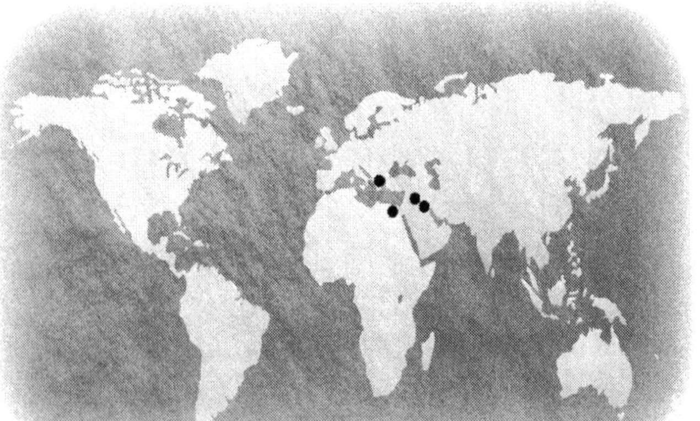

Getting your bearings

The earliest major civilisations developed from around 3,300 BC, growing out of settled rather than nomadic or small farming communities. Before this, nomadic peoples had been wandering parts of the earth for at least 500,000 years. Significantly, the new communities became established around the major rivers such as the Tigris and the Euphrates of Mesopotamia and Babylonia and the Egyptian Nile, areas important in our story But they also developed along other major rivers such as in the Indus Valley of northern India and along the Huang He (Yellow River) in western China. The predictability, and extent to which each of the rivers flooded every year, made agricultural production of food more reliable. Surplus crops were traded, extending the range of produce and materials across communities. Time could also be devoted to social, cultural and technological developments – hence the development of civilisations.

About two thousand miles away from Mesopotamia, in the middle of the Mediterranean on the island of Crete, the first European civilisation was established by the Minoans in around 2,500 BC. Other people, often migrants from the turbulent East, later settled across the Greek Islands and on the mainland of Greece.

Introduction

This chapter provides a backstory for future chapters, describing the origin of some of the ideas drawn on in the development of alchemy and related philosophical ideas and religious beliefs.

The practice of alchemy does not start until around the 3rd or 4th centuries AD, but the beliefs and methods it draws on have ancient history. The backstory to the development of alchemy is provided by exploring three contrasting civilisations - Mesopotamia, Egypt and Greece - their very different belief systems, the ways they thought about themselves and the world around them.

The First Civilisations

Of all the communities that settled along river valley areas, Egypt benefitted from having a river with the most predictable pattern of flooding, resulting in minimal destruction to life and property. From early on, the Egyptians were highly skilled technically and, from around 3,000 BC, they had advanced skills in mining, forms of chemistry and in the production and use of different types of metals, including gold, which was to be an important substance within alchemy. Metalworks also created opportunities for trade, and silver was introduced into Egypt from the Iberian Peninsula.[iv]

Another advanced Egyptian city was Heliopolis, located in the Lower Delta. This city was very influential around 2,400 BC and its priests and sages had great authority.[v] The City was a major centre of religion and learning, attracting scholars, such as Pythagoras and Plato, from within and beyond Egypt.

Mesopotamia also had large cities and Doug Metgzer describes the surprising level of sophistication cities, such as Ur, had achieved by around 2000BC.

> *"...literature, science, mathematics, state sponsored education and public works projects... consistent tax regulations and collection processes, boardinghouses that cared for women and children, state sponsored academies, weights and measures, an umbrella system for state employees that tracked, paid, and provided food for something like a million workers..."*[vi]

Early civilisations also developed systems of scripts and writing methods, emerging to accompany spoken languages. Egypt had its hieroglyphics; Mesopotamians, in cities such as Uruk, Ur and Babylon, spoke Sumerian and used cuneiform writing; Akkadians and Assyrians were Semitic speakers; and those in the Indus Valley spoke a variety of different languages and developed a common form of writing called Sanskrit.

How to Live and How to Die

Mesopotamian and Egyptian societies provide contrasting examples of ancient religions. Both societies had many gods, with just a few being particularly important. Nature's powers were not only reflected in gods of the sky/air, storms, earth but also expressed in ritual and festivals, such as those occurring before the new year's floods.[vii] The stories created and told by these ancient civilisations provided explanations and order.

The French Philosopher, Pierre Hadot (1995)[viii], believed ancient societies were characterised by two formulas: *learning to live* and a metaphysical *learning to die.*

The following section illustrates the different approaches to living and dying that Mesopotamia and Egypt adopted.

Mesopotamians created stories that combined both of elements of life and death. One thousand years before the Hebrew Bible was written, Mesopotamians had developed stories, such as The *Enuma Elish*, The *Atrahasis*[ix] *and The Epic of Gilgamesh* which conveyed their world-view. The *Enuma Elish* is a creation myth - a cosmology - telling the story of Marduk, originally the god of thunderstorms, who becomes the single lord of the gods. *The Atrahasis* tells the story of the relationship of the gods to Man. Initially the gods created Man to labour for them, but they then sent a flood when they tired of Man's rowdy and bad behaviour. Finally, to ensure that Man continued to work for the gods, they accepted a new type of relationship. Finally, the story, *He Who Saw the Deep: The Epic of Gilgamesh*, is a story of the King of Uruk and how he made sense of the world, firstly by trying to gain immortality and then, when he failed to achieve this, coming to terms with his life by finding meaning in his City and home.[x]

In a southern part of Mesopotamia, Babylonians developed their knowledge of the stars and increasingly looked upwards to read what was to come. This meant that, over time, gods became more associated with celestial bodies rather than nature. Observation of nature and the *methods* used for this resulted in prediction becoming infused with religion. Magic, divination and astrology were more developed in this society than in others.[xi]

Ironically, whilst the observation of the stars introduced a level of predictability within nature that had not previously existed, the effect this knowledge had was to reduce, rather than increase, the sense of control for those involved directly in farming and agriculture.

Olsen (1982) describes how, in Mesopotamia around 1600 BC, the monthly charting of celestial bodies had worked in tandem with agriculture seasons and related cyclical activity. Where mismatches occurred between the charts and agricultural events, adjustments were made to calendars to reflect the actual time that the inundation of the rivers and the harvests took place.

Over the following six hundred years, all the major Mesopotamian gods became associated with celestial bodies. Observation of the stars, and their patterns, had become more dominant in people's lives but these gods were clearly more detached from the basic concerns of food production. Over this six-hundred-year period, things had changed and had changed fundamentally.

By about 300 BC, the calendar of the Mesopotamians was now being laid out by priests a whole century in advance:

> *"The official religion which had once formed the most powerful unifying institution in society had gradually become the domain of a group of learned experts and had lost its intimate connection with the everyday activities of the vast bulk of men."* [xii]

Olsen explains that the grounds for a more fatalistic and horoscopic astrology became laid down and people were separated from their productive and cultural roots,

> *"…the stars and planets were gradually seen more and more as not only the messengers of the fates but also as the determiners of the fates."*[xiii]

In contrast to Mesopotamians, Egyptian philosophy and religion treated living and dying separately. Their 'wisdom literature', or moral philosophy, dealt with how to live, incorporating quite advanced ideas around ethics, fairness and law. However, they appear to have been far more concerned than the Mesopotamians with 'learning how to die', as evidenced by their 'funerary texts'.

Egypt had its regional variations of its own creation story. In Heliopolis, for example, from the self-be-gotten god Atun (later associated with the sun god Ra) nine deities were created, known as the Great Ennead.[xiv]

Death and the passage to the afterlife was highly ritualised in Egypt and administered by priests. In death, individuals faced judgement by the gods for the lives they had lived. If, after having their hearts weighed and their deeds judged (recorded by the scribe Thoth, also the god for wisdom and magic), the outcome was favourable, Egyptians believed their soul returned to the body in the afterlife; hence the need to preserve the body through mummification.[xv] Initially, this path could only be taken by the pharaohs but then, from around 1550 BC onwards, around the time when Egypt was unified and it capital became the major city of Thebes (Luxor), all followed this path; death was democratised.

Spells and incantations, believed necessary to achieve this passage, became documented in the *Book of the Dead*. From the Old Kingdom (2,686 – 2,010 BC onwards [xvi], the recording and passing on of the knowledge of how to die and how to live was to be found in every temple in a place called The **House of Life.** This was a store for religious texts, but it also functioned as a general centre of learning, containing works on subjects such as history, geography, astronomy and medicine.[xvii]

It is within Egypt that craftsmen and the priestly class developed the processes, such as metallurgy and divination, that became associated with alchemy.

The First European Civilisation

The Island of Crete is where the Minoan people created the first European civilisation. Its location within the centre of the Mediterranean made it a key location within a network of trading routes and meant that it gained many opportunities to benefit from Eastern and North African influences.

The predominance of islands and the necessity for maritime activity meant people from Greece were open to many more influences than those of the more closed communities of river valleys of Egypt and Mesopotamia. The land of the Greeks offered less reliable food production than for those around the Nile, but it did provide greater natural defences against attack and allowed its people greater freedom as they were less easily controlled by central, despotic rulers. This different experience of life gave rise to a very different culture. In Crete, for example, Minoan outlook was joyous, open and lively and it became influential in the region.

The Minoan civilisation was devasted around 1,000 BC due to some form of physical, then cultural, disruption. The weakened Minoans were overrun by invading Mycenaeans and Greeks tribes who then settled on these lands and brought influences such as scripts and alphabets, from, for example, the Phoenicians in the Levant. The new settlers absorbed aspects of Minoan culture and religion as well as creating new connections in places such as Asia Minor (Turkey) and Egypt.

New civilisations were created and over a period of around three hundred years, from the 9th to the 6th Century BC, the Greeks had established 1000 or so city states (poleis), self-governing urban centres, across mainland Greece, Crete and further afield in Sicily and Ionia. One of the most important of these Greek city states, Miletus, (in Ionia, East Turkey) is where several of the early Greek philosophers came from.[xviii]

Political rule varied over time and across the different states. Persian conquered Ionia was mainly ruled under tyrants whereas many of the city states, such as Athens, tended towards non-hereditary forms of rule and, for short periods, democracy flourished with all non-slave males participating in a government.

However, tensions between the city states became stronger, erupting into civil wars, particularly between the Spartans and Athenians. Greece became part of Alexander the Great's expansive empire which later allowed Hellenism, Greek philosophy and culture, to become influential from the West across to India. The City of Alexandria is significant for the story of alchemy and is explored in the next chapter.

Despite Alexander's success, the Greek Empire declined, succumbing to the Romans in 146 BC. Despite this defeat, Greek civilisation remained influential for many centuries after, enduring across the territories that had been part of the Hellenistic Empire.

Religion and Philosophy

As can be seen from the above description, Greek society had many more external influences compared to other advanced civilisations of the time. Maritime activity, and the freedom this provided, were important additional features shaping the outlook of this dispersed population.

An insight into the world view of the early Greeks, and their thoughts on how to live and how to die, can be found in their stories such as Homer's *The Iliad* and *The Odyssey,* stories of the Trojan War and Odysseus's return home, as well as in Hesiod's depiction of the birth of the gods in his text the *Theogony.*

Both authors are believed to have come from Asia Minor (Turkey) and their texts contain Greek and Eastern influences. Hesiod's stories of the gods have similarities with the Babylonian creation myth, the *Enûma Eliš*. The Greek gods were often aloof, and the stories are underpinned by a life governed by fate and the ceaseless, cyclical patterns of nature.[xix] However, the Greek gods were also a product of a conquering, wealthy and aristocratic imagination. There was less superstition and the gods were more human, with fewer ties to aspects of nature than the gods of other societies.

On how to die, whilst Greek religion did not share the death cult gloom of Egyptians, its religion retained belief linked to mythology.[xx] For example, a key Greek cult, were the Orphics. They probably originated around the 6th and 5th centuries BC, they worshipped the god Dionysus, the important ancient god of wine and fruitfulness, and they had beliefs linked to the underworld. The Orphics were a disciplined, ascetic sect who wanted to gain mystic knowledge and believed in the transmigration of the soul, which would then, based on its corporeal life on earth, achieve either eternal bliss or torment.

The god and men of alchemy

The gods that emerged in one civilisation could be strikingly like to those from another. For example, the Greek god Hermes appears to have similar jurisdiction over life to the Egyptian god Thoth[xxi], with both governing activities including the simple act of writing, wisdom, the mystical and impenetrable event of death and the transporting of souls to the afterlife.

As an aside, it is important to understand that alchemy has created its own mythology around the development of this practice. Some attribute the creation of alchemy to Hermes/Thoth, also known as Hermes Trismegistus (Thrice-Great Hermes). It was believed that it was his knowledge contained within two key alchemical texts, *the Corpus Hermetica* and *The Emerald Tablet.* These texts, that take the form of numerous dialogues between teacher and student, are more likely to have originated in Egypt, sometime between the 2nd and 4th centuries AD.[xxii]

One important character who appears frequently in the development of alchemy, is Pythagoras of Samos (c. 570 – c. 495 BC). Pythagoras, and the school associated with him, believed in re-incarnation. Numbers were also of central importance. The knowledge of numbers and mathematics used by this school were derived from the Egyptians and Babylonians. The Pythagoreans

> "*…regarded numbers as a fundamental aspect of reality and mathematics as a basic tool for investigating this reality.*"[xxiii]

The Pythagoreans believed in the Harmony of the Spheres, which maintained that the planets, the seven heavenly bodies, and the stars,

> "*…move according to mathematical equations, which correspond to musical notes and thus produce an inaudible symphony.*"[xxiv]

This imposition of order on nature became a hallmark of Greek Philosophy.

The Unique Greeks

The following sections look at key Greek philosophers and their ideas which are important in this unfolding story. Their thoughts around the nature of things and change provide the main focus. Plato and Aristotle are looked at in more detail given the centrality of their ideas for future systems of thinking and alchemy.

From around 600 BC, ancient philosophers from India, China, Egypt and Greece had begun building new theories that explained their world; a world that appeared to never stand still.

The Greeks went further than their predecessors when, in the 5th and 4th Centuries BC, some people began examining the nature of things in an entirely different way; through developing whole systems of philosophical thinking that both explained order, rather than just describe it, and pertain to what it means to live a good life.

Three considerations summarise the inquiries undertaken by the Greeks:

- the question of change;
- what reality is made of;
- and the problem of knowledge.[xxv]

Describing Greek systems, Warner (1958) provides an account of the originality of the Greeks by looking at the questions they asked, framed within the notion of a "cosmos", and how such questions might be answered through an orderly system governed by laws which could be discovered by logical thought and observation. He says,

> *"It would be an exaggeration to say that before the time of Thales of Miletus men were incapable of rational thought, but there would be some truth in the statement, since before his time it does not appear that anyone asked those precise questions out of which science and philosophy were to develop. The questions were "What is everything made of?", "How do things come into being, change and pass away?", "What permanent substance or sub-stances exist behind appearances?" And these questions, of course, led on to others connected with the existence of the gods, the laws of nature and the duties or purpose of man upon the earth."*[xxvi]

Within these systems of ideas, new ways of looking at the world were formed.

Change - Beyond the Gods

One dramatic shift that opened up new types of thinking about fate and the cycle of life was brought about the ideas of Xenophanes of Colophon (c. 560 BC). He questioned Hesiod's gods, such as Zeus. He posited instead that there was only one god and it had the characteristics of being all-powerful, all-knowing and all-present – omnipotence, omniscience and omnipresence. This was very unlike Zeus who, in order to influence events, had to be present and observe actions directly.

The World in Constant Change

One new way of perceiving and describing the world was by Heraclitus (535 – c. 475 BC). He believed the world was in constant change and the same thing was never repeated. Interpretations vary but his observations of nature, such as the nature of Man (waking/sleeping; young/old), led him to conclude that all existence is changing, and that long-lasting material reality exists by virtue of the constant turnover of its constituent matter. He thought that opposites are interconnected and that everything is in flux.[xxvii, xxviii] Knowledge was held in great esteem and Heraclitus deposited his book in the Temple of Artemis in Ephesus, a wonder of the ancient world, and a store of treasures and books. [xxix]

The Difference between Perception and Reality

A different view came from Parmenides (515 – 450 BC). He concluded that two worlds existed, one of reality and one of perception. For the divine, there was a changeless and eternal reality, and this existed in parallel to the one experienced by Man in which the perception of change and movement was not real but only an appearance.[xxx,, xxxi,xxxii]

The Substance of Things

Empedocles (c.490 – c. 430 BC) provided one view on what temporal reality was made from. He described four elemental and unchangeable roots - fire, earth, air and water - which combined in different ways to make reality.[xxxiii]

There were other views on what made the substance of things. One attempt to resolve these contradictory views was made by Leucippus, and then by his pupil Democritus (460 – 370 BC), who spent five years in Egypt and was an admirer of its mathematicians.

Leucippus and Democritus proposed that all matter was composed of small indivisible particles called atoms. They provided theories on how material substances are created, and relationships between decay, change, space and voids.[xxxiv] This view challenged any notion of divinity as it explained the world as a product of random and mechanistic reactions of atoms in relation to each other. This thinking became associated much later on with materialism[xxxv] epicureanism and atomism.[xxxvi]

The Universe and The Uniqueness of Man.

Two philosophers, Plato and Aristotle, were inspired by many of the ideas of the philosophers from Greece that came before them. Plato also credited others from further afield, acknowledging, for example, that the wisdom of the ages had been preserved in Egypt.[xxxvii] In his *Timeaus*, he credited Egyptian priests, amongst others, with having a superior knowledge to that of his fellow Greeks. Plato and Aristotle incorporated many of these earlier ideas into their own systems, integrating the heavenly cosmos and the earthly worlds. They investigated the uniqueness of Man, how to run a good society, the relationships between people. They also created the methods by which such knowledge should be developed.

Plato

Platonic ideas, or a version of them, are central to much of the development of alchemy. The central concept within Plato (428 – 322 BC) is that our world is an imperfect copy of a higher world – that is, the world of the Forms which he describes in *The Republic.* Plato's system of ideas was developed over his lifetime through multiple works. Some of his ideas on the Forms, may well have been inspired by Egyptian concepts.[xxxviii]

Plato believed that the aim of human existence was to come to know the ideal, universal essences (Form/idea), a world that is separate from the one we inhabit. In developing the idea of the Forms, Plato was also inspired by the conceptual ideas developed by the Pythagoreans. They saw that, although numbers were concepts, concepts also existed as a non-material aspect of reality. For example, the concept of a perfect circle exists in the imagination, but a perfect circle cannot exist as a reality. Plato concluded that a separate world of ideal Forms must therefore also exist. For Plato, these ideal Forms were of Being, Beauty, Goodness, Equality, Bigness, Unity, Likeness, Sameness, Difference, Change, and Changelessness. Man should aim for this higher knowledge rather than squandering his time on pursuing the more immediate, earthly impressions of these things.

Plato describes the creation of these separate worlds in *The Timaeus* (the only work of Plato's available in the West until medieval times). Here, unlike The Creation by the God of medieval theologians, Plato thought the creation of the universe was undertaken by the 'Demiurge', not from nothing (ex nihilo),

> "*...but rather orders the cosmos out of chaotic elemental matter, imitating the eternal Forms.*[xxxix]

His *Timaeus* is also a detailed work on the natural world and the disciplines of physics, astronomy, chemistry and biology required to understand it.

> *"Plato takes the four elements, fire, air, water, and earth (which Plato proclaims to be composed of various aggregates of triangles), making various compounds of these into what he calls the Body of the Universe."*[xl]

The spiritual element of Plato, inspired by Orphic/ Pythagorean ideas, is his concept of the soul, the place where knowledge of the forms resides. The soul is key for how Plato believed knowledge is gained. The soul, when unencumbered by a person's body, is better able to know the Forms.

> *"The soul always retains the ability to recollect what it once grasped of the forms, when it was disembodied prior to its possessor's birth [see especially The Meno], and that the lives we lead are to some extent a punishment or reward for choices we made in a previous existence."*[xli]

He believed that the knowledge that resides in a person, exists already as an impression on the soul within his body. So, Man's knowledge exists a *priori*, and it is recollection that allows this knowledge to be rediscovered, yet always in its imperfect form.

Plato also believed that the soul is divided into a rational part (that loves truth and should use reason to rule over the other parts of the soul); a spirited part (which loves honour and victory); and an appetitive part (which desires food, drink, and sex). Each must do its own work.[xlii] This is the basis for Plato's moral philosophy and gives rise to his conclusion that moral weakness can occur when one part of the soul chooses to overrule the work of another.

Politics for Plato was about how Man conducts himself within the real world. He discussed his ideal of how life should be in *The Republic* and then, at a more practical and detailed level in *The Laws,* believed to be his final work. His creation of the fictitious cities, Kallipolis and Magnesia, found respectively in *The Republic* and *The Laws,* allow him to describe how these ideals can be realised in the day to day life of its citizens as they interact in their different roles.

Given the imperfect world we inhabit, Plato considered the methods by which we acquire knowledge and how it is possible to come to know the real Forms. The legacy Plato leaves is partly the openness of his inquiring method, Socratic debate and the process of "collection and division." Describing Plato's openness, Kraut (2017) says,

> "*One of his deepest methodological convictions (affirmed in Meno, Theaetetus, and Sophist) is that in order to make intellectual progress we must recognize that knowledge cannot be acquired by passively receiving it from others: rather, we must work our way through problems and assess the merits of competing theories with an independent mind.*"[xliii]

Plato was not providing a blueprint, but a method and set of persuasive arguments he believed established a truth about the world - he also believed it was then necessary for the reader to judge for themselves whether they were convinced by the case put forward.

Aristotle and the Problem of Knowledge

Like Plato, Aristotle (384 – 322 BC) is central to the story of the development of alchemy and he was also influenced and inspired by many of the ideas of the philosophers that came before him.

> *"Human beings began to do philosophy even as they do now, because of wonder, at first because they wondered about the strange things right in front of them, and then later, advancing little by little, because they came to find greater things puzzling"* (Met. 982b12)[xliv].

But of the many areas of study undertaken by his predecessors, the discussions about the nature of change particularly fascinated Aristotle.

Like Plato, Aristotle thought that testing and the proof of knowledge should be achieved through teaching, discussion, clarification and persuasion. Before he could draw his own conclusions from the work of others, he needed to test these theories and work out which ones could be proved to be true.

This aspect of Aristotle is important. It is Aristotle's logic, and associated methodologies, that are deployed over future centuries in contests of truth and in establishing what ideas should be orthodoxies and which were heresies.

Man's ability to reason drove Aristotle's search for methods and tools aiding this activity. He attributed different status to types of knowledge, and he set out varying types of logical reasoning appropriate to different types of problems. He developed a rigorous method of logic, allowing him to look again at material reality. As knowledge was of different types, each required different methods of inquiry - deductive reasoning, scientific presentation and dialectical reasoning.

His methodology, encompassing theoretical sciences practical sciences, and productive sciences provided distinct branches of knowledge that could, importantly, be taught, tested and passed on.

The body of methods and tools he created to demonstrate truth later became known as the Organon which included works on deductive reasoning *(The Categories, Prior Analytics*), on the demands of scientific presentation *(The Posterior Analytics*) and on dialectical reasoning (*The Topics*). He took account of, and valued, the contributions made by previous theories. Using dialectics, for example, he judged which aspects of past inherited received wisdom (Endoxa) continued to be valid.

Aristotle's generated his own view on the essential nature of reality and change; a method for categorising different types of being, such as its substance, quality and quantity, and the relationship between the matter of things and the form of things. He agreed on the four elements but also believed a fifth existed from which the celestial heavenly bodies were made.[xlv]

Aristotle contested the dualist theory of Plato who believed there was a separation between form and matter. In *The Physics,* Aristotle explores the principles of nature, concluding that what something becomes, emerges from its opposite - such as a seed into a plant or a baby into a man. He concluded that the form of something must be present in the original matter, with matter being the constant factor.

His explanatory scheme set out the four causes[xlvi] of being.

The Four Causes

The *material* cause is the matter that makes something up
The *formal* cause is a thing's shape or form
The *efficient* cause creates a thing
The *final* (first) cause is that thing's purpose

He believed that this process, regardless of whether or not the end purpose was created by design, is driven towards an end purpose (teleology).

He was the first person to develop a systematic study of biology. He examined the features and characteristics of Man and animals and what made them different. He believed that the intrinsic goodness and knowledge of things was gained, initially, through the sense perception of the world as it is experienced. And he concluded that the uniqueness of Man was his ability to reason, a characteristic that defined his humanity.[xlvii]

> *"Aristotle reasoned that humans must have a function specific to humans, and that this function must be an activity of the soul in accordance with reason."*[xlviii]

Aristotle created a hierarchical view of the universe in which there was a sharp distinction between the sublunar, imperfect, finite world of change, and the eternal and immutable celestial bodies making up the heavens. This distinction was to become thoroughly tested from the Renaissance onwards.

Aristotle's conception of the City that men inhabit was an organic one, closely tied to his work on physics[xlix] in which he conceived of politics as being like

> *"...an organism rather than like a machine, and as a collection of parts none of which can exist without the others. Aristotle's conception of the city is organic, and he is considered one of the first to conceive of the city in this manner".*[l]

Like Plato, Aristotle also considered ethics. However, his conceptions of ethics were more practical than theoretical. His approach was not to develop knowledge for its own sake but, through education, to pursue an end which concerned itself with *becoming* and *doing* good.

However, both philosophers ultimately believed in the existence of something external or greater than matter and life – a separate world or universe of perfect forms - that has, as a whole, some purpose in its own right.

Olsen (1982) indicates that, for Aristotle, there was a limit in Man's capacity compared to what lay beyond him,

> *"Aristotle had insisted that the subject matters of the most dignified "theoretical" sciences were beyond human capacity to alter in any way, and that knowledge not aimed at action is the most blessed and divine of human acquisitions. "* [li]

This chapter has provided some contrasting examples of how early civilisations saw themselves and made sense of their world. By the time of Alexander the Great, wars, development and trade resulted in many different and competing ideas being flung together. Greek philosophy was a significant step forward as it developed a number of distinct ways of thinking about the world and methodologies for how to think about these different problems. Greek philosophy provided some of the key foundations and raw materials for others to work with for the following two thousand years.

Several lines of inquiry became the enduring themes for future societies - developing an explanatory system of nature and its secrets, who should undertake this voyage of discovery, how should this be done and how far should this be take.

CHAPTER TWO

THE CITY OF THE MIND and THE UNIVERSAL LIBRARY

WHEN and WHERE

336 - 31 BC

ALEXANDRIA

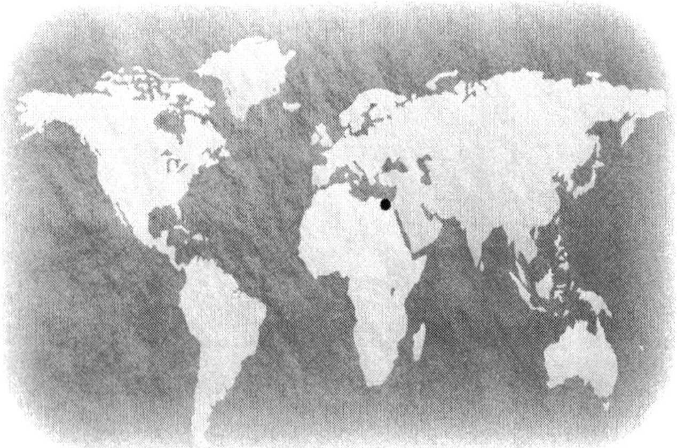

Getting your Bearings

Under the military leadership of the Macedonian general, Alexander, the Greek Empire incorporated most of the Greek territories in the West and across to the Indus Valley, India, in the East.

Although the region was often consumed in battles between, for example, the Greeks, Sumerians, Persians, Egyptians and Babylonians, conflict also brought about religious and cultural exchange. Many gods, a single god, free will, good and evil, magic spells, angels and demons, divination, reaching the afterlife, were amongst the mixture of ideas at large in Greek society. Zoroastrianism, a religion from Persia, incorporating ritual and magic and practised by the ancient priests called Magi, is one example of a religion influencing early Greek philosophers. Trade was also important, and the maritime Greeks, inquisitive and open, assimilated influences from different civilisations. In addition, many philosophers actively sought ideas, travelling, for example, to Egypt.

After Alexander's victory over the Persians in Syria, Egypt was conquered with little resistance, partly because this released Egyptians from the harsh Persian rule they had been under.

Observation (astronomy) and Bronze Age technological advances continued to develop alongside wars, conquest and military alliances.

Introduction

This chapter focuses on the Egyptian city, Alexandria. It is important for our story for two reasons. The City was one of the most important places of learning in the ancient world, famously known for its enormous library. Second, it was the city that became a key centre of alchemy.

Alexandria was established out of the vision Alexander the Great had for it. Located between the East and the West, it became a magnet, drawing many people to it. Ancient Egyptian religion, ideas from the East and from Greek philosophy melded to form new beliefs. Alexandria become an incubator for ideas that spread across the Hellenistic Empire.

City of the Mind - The Idea of Universal Knowledge

The rapid growth of the Greek Empire under Alexander took place over the seventeen years of his rule. This was achieved by a whole mixture of approaches, from total brutality to diplomacy. And to help consolidate his rule, Alexander constructed or developed a number of major cities.

It is important to note that Alexander, and his friend Ptolemy who later became a ruler of Egypt, had both been pupils of Aristotle.

Although, in his early years, Alexander was strongly influenced by Aristotle, his beliefs evolved, influenced by a mix of ideas and beliefs. Greek cities became magnets for people from across the Empire, helping to consolidate Greek rule, but also introducing new ideas brought from different places.

Alexander, whether bestowed upon him by others or by himself, became a divine and worshipped figure. It was in the city of Alexandria, in Egypt, where built the grandest of cities. The Megalopolis / Cosmopolis he envisaged would be constructed differently to those of the Greek city state model.[lii] Alexander also believed that through his construction of a new type of city, he would break down the cultural superiority assumed by the Greeks.[liii]

Aristotle had overseen a survey, undertaken by his students, of 158 of the 1000[liv] Greek city-states. He had concluded that there were certain features and conditions necessary for a good society. From this, he believed that the city Alexander envisaged would be impossible to govern because of the size and diversity of the population. [lv]

Bertrand Russell (1946) argued that, although philosophically, the concept of cosmopolitanism arises with the Stoics, in practice, it began with Alexander.[lvi]

It was not Alexander, but his commander, Cleomenes, who began building the city. The location of the new city provided a large port which was key for trade and defence, making it strategically and economically important. Egypt also had a reliable and plentiful food supply, aided by the predictable flooding of the Nile.

A significant feature and landmark of the new City was the building of a library that would allow the pursuit of virtue; good through reason. The library became the largest in the known world. Egypt's tradition of temple-based libraries was a long-established institution.[lvii] However, in contrast to many of the Egyptian libraries, which were secretive and closed to outsiders, Alexander's library would be open for *all* scholarship and learning.

The library at Alexandria was to provide a new turning point in Hellenism, serving as a collective focal point for scholars, both bringing together and dispersing ideas and learning. It was also the first of its kind, aiming to contain all existing knowledge.

Alexander was not to witness the realisation of his vision as the building of the great library did not begin until after his death. The building of the library was begun under Ptolemy I Soter (c 297 BC), who was advised by Demetrius of Phaleron, a philosopher from the Greek Peripatetic School, and completed by Ptolemy II (285-246 BCE). In a letter from the 2nd century BC, it seems that the library was conceived as a universal library:

> *"Demetrius...had at his disposal a large budget in order to collect, if possible, all the books in the world;...to the best of his ability, he carried out the king's objective. (Letters 9–10.)"*[lviii]

Invitations for the opening of the library were sent to rulers and scholars asking them to contribute books to this new institution. Most of the items were bought, but other means were sometimes used - such as searching all ships entering the harbour.[lix]

A Museum added a new dimension to the library, becoming a magnet for scholars from across the whole region to meet and work together.[lx] This centre created a movement of ideas and stimulated an unprecedented level of research, including the examination of the qualities of the earth and its inhabitants[lxi] and over time and indexing of this knowledge by Galen.[lxii] In the words of Mason, Alexandria became a **City of the Mind.**[lxiii]

The culture forged through this experimental city-building was then exported back out into the Greek empire. The Ptolemaic library remained a focal point for many years[lxiv] and some of the examples below illustrate how important Alexandria was as a centre of learning.

Calculating the World – Astronomy, Geometry and Mathematics

Alexandria's museum, containing a small observatory, acted as a catalyst for developments in calculation and measurement. Several scholars used mathematics and physics in their work. Some used a text on geometry compiled by Euclid, a highly regarded mathematician who taught in Alexandria. Euclid's best-known and extremely influential book, *Elements*, contained four hundred and sixty-five carefully presented geometry propositions and proofs.

One astronomer, Aristarchus of Samos, arrived at two significant scientific conclusions during his time in Alexandria. In one conclusion, he estimated the Sun was at least three hundred times larger than the Earth. Second, he also proposed that the Earth and the other planets revolve around the Sun. His second conclusion was not accepted. Instead, it was the calculations and the views of Alexandria's renowned astronomer, Ptolemy, that the Earth, not the Sun, was at the centre of the universe system, that was accepted, a view prevailing for the next fourteen centuries.

In a further scientific development, Eratosthenes, the director of the Alexandrian Library, tried to estimate the Earth's size. Using geometry, he calculated that the Earth's circumference was between 28,000 and 29,000 miles. Modern measurements put the circumference at 24,860 miles.

Another important Hellenistic scientist, Archimedes of Syracuse, studied at Alexandria. He accurately estimated the value of pi (π)—the ratio of the circumference of a circle to its diameter. He also used his genius for practical applications such as the building of a large boat and the development of tools such as the Archimedes Screw used to move quantities of water.[lxv]

Alchemy's Centre

In addition to Alexandria being a centre of learning and scholarship, it also became, in time, a major centre for alchemy.

Alexander had encouraged traditional Egyptian religion and there was a flourishing of interest in the incantations, magic and spells that went with funerary ritual, as found in the Book of the Dead. Religious influences around personal salvation, rebirth, and immortality were promised by mystery cults and Babylonian priests peddled astrology and divination, diminishing the status of the bank of astronomical expertise and the data that had been accumulated.

Within the great city of Alexandria, the merging of Egyptian and Greek belief systems lay the basis for alchemy. As mentioned in the first chapter, Egyptian alchemy was said to have begun with the Greek/Egyptian god, Thoth or Hermes Trismegistus.

For the Greeks, according to Pliny's account, the legendary figure, Ostanes, sometimes called the 'Father of alchemy' was said to have accompanied Xerxes during the second Persian invasion of Greece 480–479 BC, introducing the Greeks to written accounts of Persian magic.[lxvi] The writings of Ostanes are said to the be first accounts of alchemy, with some seeing him as possessing knowledge of the philosophers stone.

Empire

Alexander's conquests had geographically united western and eastern territories, including present-day Syria, Iraq and Iran, with the city of Alexandria being located at its centre. The newly conquered Empire was consolidated through the creation of garrisons and dozens of cities, many of them also called Alexandria.[lxvii] This allowed for the creation of an administrative network across the Empire, connected through the Greek language, ensuring effective communication trade and scholarship. After the death of Alexander, the Greek language, ideas and customs continued to be established throughout the Empire. This was aided by the scholarship developed through the library and museum at Alexandria, ruled by the Ptolemaic kings of Egypt and supported by the remaining network of generals (Diadochi) and administrators.[lxviii]

The spread of Greek influence, Hellenism, ensured that important aspects of the Greek spirit of inquiry were preserved and spread, with some people advancing ideas that had previously been rejected:

> "*Babylonia was much more profoundly influenced by Hellenism. As we have seen, the only ancient who followed Aristarchus of Samos in maintaining the Copernican system was Seleucus of Seleucia on the Tigris, who flourished about 150 BC.*"[lxix]

However, despite the efforts of scholars, the monarchs and generals that increasingly controlled society began to exert a conservative influence, lessening freedom of expression and any challenges to their authority.[lxx] For example, they discouraged the writing of the irreverent political poetry that had been central to this art, making it unwise for people to write about political themes or poke fun at the powerful.

The philosophical ideas upon which earlier, republican Greek civilisation had developed came under further pressure as people moved within the Empire. Wider social changes also took place and elements of different religions were absorbed into each other. Politics and scholarship declined significantly, and the religious outlook of personal salvation was becoming a strong current in society and, over time, would undermine the republican ideas of civic virtue.[lxxi]

The historical moment that saw the creation of Alexandria and the library and the melding of contradictory beliefs from Egypt, Greece, Mesopotamia, Persia and Anatolia is understood by many as a cultural achievement but also one that was understood by some as being problematic for the underpinning philosophical ideas of Greek society.

Writing in the 1940s, Bertrand Russell commented,

> *"It had the result that the interaction of Greek and barbarian was reciprocal; the barbarians learnt something of Greek science; while the Greeks learnt much of barbarian superstition.*

> *Greek civilisation, in covering a wider area, became less purely Greek.*"[lxxii]

For Russell, this process had a negative impact on Greek thought as the mystical ideas of Babylonians and Chaldeans became very influential on the Greek imagination. He argued that due to the influences of Eastern civilisations, with their antiquity, wisdom, astrology and magic, even the best Greek philosophers fell in with the belief of astrology.[lxxiii]

However, despite this decline, the imprint of philosophical ideas based on reason continued to evolve with new schools emerging[lxxiv] including Epicureanism and stoicism.[lxxv]

One example, indicating the continued influence of Aristotle's approach that included study and observation was the 3rd Century BC Greek/Roman Empiric School. This school held that that practice (in their case medical) should develop through observation and experience and that theory is an *outcome* of medical observation and experience, not its origin.[lxxvi]

Other strands were less free-thinking and open, tending towards a more rigid philosophy. Sometimes this became little more than pragmatic guidance for day to day actions. An acceptance of order also developed with, for example, Stoicism, taking people down the path of acceptance of natural hierarchy.[lxxvii]

Alexandria and its library had created a bold vision – the idea and possibility that everything could be known and the creation of a store of universal knowledge. This provided a tantalising challenge, driving philosophers, scholars and alchemists forward for centuries.

CHAPTER THREE

THE TEMPLE OF LIBERTY
to
THE CITY OF GOD

WHEN and WHERE

146 BC – AD 700

CONSTANTINOPLE • ROME • ALEXANDRIA

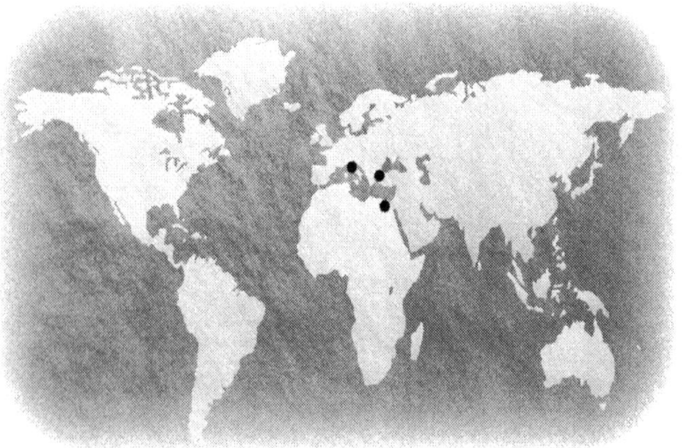

Getting your bearings

In the 8th century BC, Italy became subject to the external influences of the more advanced civilisations of the Etruscans in the North of the Country and the Greeks in the South. Rome, a burgeoning agricultural centre, based around the crossing point of the River Tiber, became subject to rule by Etruscan kings. These kings were then unseated by influential Roman families, the Patricians. Rome was faced with many internal conflicts; these being partly resolved through it becoming a republic around 510 BC.

There was also upheaval in Greece at the same time. In the same year of 510 BC, an Athenian tyrant fell due to an Athenian alliance made with the Spartans. Over the next few centuries, the influence of Rome extended across the whole peninsula. Dealing with threats to its authority, Rome centralised power, and Augustus Caesar became emperor in 27 BC. By this time, Rome had established an empire, encompassing Sicily, Sardinia, Corsica, most of Spain, Macedonia, parts of northern Africa and the lands of Pergamum in Asia Minor.

Introduction

It was during the period of the creation of the Roman Empire that many new cult-religions emerged. It was also under the Empire that alchemy emerged as a practice, alongside mystics, cults, Christianity and philosophers.

This chapter sets out some of the key features of Roman life and its culture, the gradual change in state religion from paganism to Christianity and describes the key new cults.

Roman Culture

Although the Greeks were defeated by the Romans in 146 BC, the influence of their culture within the late Roman Republic was evident within the Roman gods, arts, philosophy and education. The Greek army had carried the Greek language across their empire[lxxviii] and varieties of this language had become the dominant lingua franca, adopted within Roman public life alongside Latin.

However, the adoption of Greek intellectual ideas was not fully embraced. For example, in the later period of the Roman Republic, Roman censors closed the schools of Latin rhetoric in Rome in 92 BC and those interested in serious study, such as Cicero, who became the influential lawyer, stateman and orator, went East, in his case, to Athens.[lxxix] In addition, when the Hellenistic kingdoms were being dismantled by the Romans, Greek scholars moved to Hellenistic centres such as Naples.[lxxx]

Whilst the Romans forged their own ideas, particularly in the fields of city planning, transport, trade and imports and the law, they also created a hierarchy of important and lesser ideas between themselves and the Greeks. Romans were concerned with the important subjects of oratory, law and history, incorporating dialectics whilst Greek scholars taught the 'lesser' subjects, including medicine and architecture. Greek slaves also provided the skills for teaching and the copying of manuscripts.[lxxxi]

Roman society and culture were bound together with a strong sense of tradition and belonging based around the family and grounded within the militaristic, Trojan War foundation myth. This Roman culture created a magnetic pull, drawing in those from outside its boundaries needing a haven from other, much more hostile places.[lxxxii]

The status of libraries within Roman life is one way of charting the importance of knowledge and scholarship within this society.

Libraries were to become a feature of Roman life. Private ones were created first with these dating back to the 1st and 2nd centuries BC. Roman general, Lucius Aemilius Paulus (229 – 160 BC), for example, plundered all the books from the library of the defeated King Perseus, in the Third Macedonian War, creating his own private collection in Rome.[lxxxiii]

Fielden (2001) writes that the first Roman public library appears to have been built by historian Gaius Asinius Pollio (75 BC – AD 4) and it was located in the Hall or **Temple of Liberty** [lxxxiv],

> *"G. Asinius Pollio probably brought together several collections from other Romans of note, such as Varro's and Sulla's, and founded the first public library in Rome, at the Temple of Liberty in 39 BC. He probably used the booty from the wars against the Parthini to accomplish this."*[lxxxv]

And the Roman, Pliny the Elder (AD 23–79), said of Pollio,

> *"...he was the first to make men's talents public property..."*[lxxxvi]

In the period of the first Emperor, Augustus Caesar, politics was a robust and dangerous affair, but the arts, libraries and literature also flourished under Caesar's patronage. This patronage continued under other emperors too and resulted in an intense period of creativity producing writers such as Lucretius, Cicero, Horace, Virgil, Ovid, Livy and Seneca.[lxxxvii]

Greek culture, including its philosophy of substance and change and its mythology, were hugely influential on this literature. But the Roman's also contributed their own innovations. The poet and philosopher Lucretius adopted the ideas of the atomist, Democritus, who saw the world as being made up of colliding, mechanistic atoms, and the associated philosophy of the Epicureans.[lxxxviii] Ovid, used the notion of change as a theme in his *Metamorphosis*, weaving in the philosophical, ever-changing, world of Heraclitus and the belief in reincarnation of Pythagoras.[lxxxix]

Roman Religion

Greek and Roman cultures both had polytheistic religions with many gods. Roman rule, grounded in this system of beliefs, kept peace with the gods who influenced life and nature, through its rituals and ancestral traditions.

A Civic Imperial Cult was established during the reign of Consul and Dictator, Julius Caesar. Divinity became established as an integral feature of office and, at some point around the first century, the Cult of Mithras emerged. The Cult supported the Emperor, valued the bond of brotherhood and the Italian Roman soldiers, who mainly practised it, usually did so in secret and often in underground caves.

There were also several external religious influences on Roman civilisation. As with the Greek Empire, conquest also brought about the intermingling of different societies, bringing many new influences into the West. Religions such as Zoroastrianism (from Persia), Manichaeism (from Baghdad) and Buddhism (from India) spread to the countries of the Mediterranean and the wider Roman Empire.

The Emergence of Monotheism

Some of these religions challenged the belief systems in the West. For example, Zoroastrianism believed in one primary god of goodness contending against a lesser god of evil and any setbacks in goodness were temporary. The former resided in heaven and the latter in hell. Judaism, emerging in the Levant area, was probably influenced by the Zoroastrianism, becoming the first truly monotheistic religion following the period of Jewish exile in Babylonia. Judaism spread to Egypt and throughout the Roman-ruled Mediterranean. It was during the emerging conflicts between the Jewish Kingdom and Roman rule that the roots of Christianity developed.

The form of Roman rule had an impact on some territories within the Empire. Their imposition of centralised power located in Rome disrupted, for example, the natural order established in the Greek city states, reflected in Greek thinking and reasoned philosophy.[xc] This was experienced by Greek citizens as a loss of control and was one factor resulting in rebellion against Roman rule. Sidentop (2014) argues that rebellion was also to be found in new a religion, Christianity, which had a single divine and powerful god, mirroring and competing with the power of Rome.

> *"It was as if the trials of dealing with Roman power were being projected on to a universal screen. Was 'will' rather than 'reason' the key to things? If so, could a philosophical tradition that*

> *presented reasons as the key both to nature and to right living provide an adequate conception of the will?"*[xci]

An alternative power now contented with Rome where, as Sidentop says,

> *"...the categories of mind could, in a sense, 'command' reality, even when that involved defining an immutable order or 'fate'."*[xcii]

By the 3rd and 4th centuries, several factors, including economic problems and plague contributed to a period of instability, putting the whole Imperial Cult at risk. There were now new contenders in the domain of universal truths.

As their authority was challenged, the rulers of the Roman Empire developed an uneasy and conflicted relationship with magical, pagan and Christian religions. The 4th Century was significant with a dramatic change of official belief taking place over the course of the Century.

At the start of this century, in AD 303, Emperor Diocletian demonstrated his commitment to his polytheistic religion through his persecution of the *Christians.* It was believed, for example, that Christian refusal to make sacrifices to the gods might weaken Roman authority and undermine its civic imperial cult. In an attempt at re-ordering society around traditional Roman pagan practices, each of the different Emperors during this century issued decrees resulting in the persecution of Christians.

Such persecutions were not entirely new, and such tensions existed previously. For example, in 139 BC, Chaldean astrologers were expelled from Rome by Praetor Cornelius Hispallus, and magic was outlawed under Roman law.

However, by the 4th Century, the Roman Empire faced graver threats as it tried to manage its extensive empire and resist new challenges at its borders.

A shift from pagan polytheism to Christian monotheism began. The 4th century opened with a persecution of Christians but ended with a decree against the Pagans.

When Constantine became Emperor in AD 306, he reunified the Empire, creating a new capital at Constantinople and converting to Christianity. The polytheistic paganism became viewed as backward, practised mainly by peasants. In AD 380, Theodosius I established Christianity as the Empire's state religion, creating an Empire led by a single ruler under a single god.

In AD 391 Theodosius proscribed *pagan* religious practices and their places of worship were closed down. Pagans facing persecution and possible death were cut off from their ancestors, traditions and their past. The impact of this can be understood symbolically. The eternal flame for the goddess Vesta, that had burned in temples since the 8th century BC, was extinguished. One can only imagine how this single measure might have fomented deep anxieties, disorientating many. But for Rome, this move represented a new consolidation of its power, helping to maintain its rule.

It is important to note that in the early centuries of the Roman Empire, theological debates against heretical elements were not always conducted in ways resulting in physical punishment or expulsion. Rather, the counter-position of different beliefs in debate allowed the central tenets of Christian orthodoxy to be clarified and its foundations more firmly established.

Despite Rome's efforts, it continued to be challenged.

Cults of Rome

The next sections describe four of the many new cults, religions and practices challenging Rome's authority. Alchemy was one of these practice.

Christianity and its Cults

An emphasis on revelation within some religions grew, and the quest for knowledge became linked to a dualistic world-view with the spirit seeking to detach itself from an imperfect material world and to be united with a higher being. Such mystical belief was adopted within the outgrowths of Christianity, such as within Gnosticism whose most important centre was in Alexandria.[xciii]

The Egyptian Gnostic, Valentinus, born around the year AD 100, was educated in Alexandria and created an academy, which in turn formed a loose network of local groups. Attaining knowledge became linked to forms of divination and magic and Christian esotericism.[xciv] Valentius had a very large following that spread across the empire.[xcv] Christian Gnosticism, and Cynicism, which came before it, shunned the material world, reflected in their belief in a dualistic order with a good and superior spiritual world and evil imperfect temporal world, flawed by foolish error during its creation (also a feature of Zoroastrianism).

The side-stepping of priests, where spiritual mysteries could be attained through empirical knowledge, was also found in non-Christian Gnosticism and Hermeticism. There was also Jewish Kabbalah that was concerned with God's essence.

Philosophic religion

Wildberg (2016) explains that a natural theology, arising from a synthesis of classical philosophy and religions, emerged from around the mid-3rd century AD, creating:

> *"…a grandiose and powerfully persuasive system of thought that reflected upon a millennium of intellectual culture and brought the scientific and moral theories of Plato, Aristotle, and the ethics of the Stoics into fruitful dialogue with literature, myth, and religious practice."*[xcvi]

Ancient philosophers, such as Socrates and Aristotle, had identified a unique ability within Man that was distinct from other animals; his capacity to *reason* to gain an understanding of the material world. This was made possible by his ability to determine knowledge which was grounded in sense perception and logic. It was in the nature of Man to seek a good earthly life through pursuit of knowledge of the *sensible* earthly realm.

However, Plato emphasised the *intelligible other worldly* realm. Plotinus (c. AD 204/5– 270), who was from Egypt, studied in Alexandria and spoke Greek, crafted a new interpretation of Greek Classical philosophy. He took elements from, for example, Plato's *Timaeus*, *The Republic* and *The Parmenides* and from Aristotle's *De Anima* and *The Metaphysics*, creating the concept of The One (from Aristotle's Unmoved Mover). He synthesised these with other concepts from, for example, Gnosticism.[xcvii]

Within this process of synthesising, taking from philosophy, physics and metaphysics, there was a clear shift of focus within the traditions of Greek philosophy towards theology, god and the nature of the divine.[xcviii]

Although Christianity influenced philosophers, there were disputes. These rationalist philosophers took issue with influential Christians, believing their many biblical historical inaccuracies showed them to be irrational.[xcix] There were also disputes *between* philosophers on the nature of revelation of God to man. Porphyry (c. AD 234 – 305), for example, who studied with Plotinus in Rome, strove to retain part of the classical tradition where; '*only reason, exercised by a pure mind, could lead to unity with the One God*'. This compares to other philosophers, like Iamblichus (AD 245 - 325), who competed with the Christians, by endowing pagan ideas with authority and superiority through their association with ancient ideas like the Chaldean ritual practice of theurgy (the process for the transmutation of substances to assist internal revelation).[c]

This mix of ancient philosophical schools, established in Athens and Alexandria, with their practising pagan professors, continued up to the early 6th century.

Mystery Religions

In addition to imperial cults, old pagan religions, such as the cultic magic of private and public rituals and practices of healing and divination[ci], remained influential. Practices from Egyptian alchemy were adopted (see below). And new practices, such as Hermeticism, formed from a synthesis of Egyptian and Greek writing and philosophy.[cii] [ciii].

Hermeticism is based on a mythological teacher, the ancient Egyptian god Hermes Trismegistus, whose teachings are said to have been found within the collection of hermetic writings, known by some as *The Emerald Tablet* (believed to have been written during this period rather than originating much earlier). Greek Christian theologian, Clement of Alexandria (AD 150 – 215) referred to this text and,

> *"... was under the impression that the Egyptians had forty-two sacred writings by Hermes, encapsulating all the training of Egyptian priests.*[civ]

Hermeticism utilised many ancient texts and practices, including alchemy and magic, as well as influences from the Jewish Kabbalah, Pythagorean or Chaldean numerology and Babylonian astrology.

Goodrick-Clarke (2008), examining esotericism, he explains that within the Corpus Hermeticum humans had a divine intellect, unlike Judaism and Christianity that believed God to be beyond human comprehension. With this divine intellect humans

> *"...could reflect the whole universe in their minds. The theme of the divine intellect as a "mirror," on which "speculating" is a continuous exchange with higher spiritual entities, is a major theme of esotericism. Because God created the universe, it is saturated with his spiritual symbols. Once humans learn to read these symbols, they can know God directly. In this way, Hermeticism negates any absolute ontological dualism between God and his Creation."* [cv]

These new influences could also be problematic for those in official power. For example, while the use of astrology in Egyptian society had been used to predict the inundation of the Nile, this ability also gave the priests (and the associated gods) great power. This power, and the practices associated with it, sat uneasily with the rulers of the Roman Empire. The result of this was the expulsion from Rome of the Chaldean astrologers in 139 BC and in magic being declared punishable by death in AD 199.

Early Alchemy

It is in this period that alchemy began to flourish – initially as an artisanal process that experimented with copying material. For example, fragments of text by the Roman Egyptian Agathodaimaon (c. AD 300) survive, describing the use of certain elements and minerals to produce silver. It is likely that these artisans kept their recipes and results as trade 'secrets'. This later became a quest to turn base metals into noble ones (such as to gold).

Miriam the Jewess, possibly a mythical, composite character of the ancient world, moved amongst the philosophers who were making systematic observations of the world. She is associated with creating instruments of experimentation and with developing new ways to process natural substances, including grinding and calcination, and for creating substances such as hydrochloric acid. Pseudo-Democritus, a 2nd-century AD Greek philosopher begins to introduce references to shadowy magical practices, marking a shift in how experimentation was considered by some.[cvi]

Experimental processes were then fused with Greek philosophical theories on *what* matter was made of and alchemy became a concept in its own right.[cvii] The oldest surviving alchemical text is by the Gnostic Zosimos of Panopolis (AD 280) who conducted real-world experiments, believing in metallic transmutation, turning lead into silver, copper and gold. His experimental process was a transformative one, bringing about changes in physical objects while being, simultaneously, a search for oneness with an external divine god.

> *"The priest, this man of copper...he has changed the color of his nature and has become a man of silver. If thou wishest, thou wilt soon have him a man of gold."*[cviii]

Thus, the act of contemplating the transformation achieved during a physical process is, at the same time, how the inner world achieves purification and redemption (known as theurgy originating from Babylonian Chaldean astrologers).

Alchemy was perceived to be a major threat, partly because of magic, but also due to Emperor Diocletian's concerns that successful experiments in gold production risked further economic instability within the Empire. Diocletian moved against the alchemists around AD 297 when he attempted to destroy alchemy's literary heritage, reportedly ordering all

> *"books written by the Egyptians on the cheimeia of silver and gold" to be burned."*[cix]

The many competing ideas described above are indicative of the erosion of Rome's strength and power. The competing ideas and religions contributed to and were a product of this decline. From its first century zenith, the second, third and fourth centuries brought gradual degradation, economic decline, civil war and invasion. Territories were lost, such as those to the Palmyrene Empire, and some areas, like the Gallic state, developed their independence. The power within the Empire shifted away from Imperial Romans to military generals from Spain in the West and the Germanic peoples of the East. There were attempts by Rome to halt this decline, including the creation of more emperors governing smaller areas such as the Western and Eastern empires.

This dispersal of power did not lead to the development of new rational philosophical ideas, as might have happened;[cx] instead, Roman culture declined.

Looking again at libraries, we return to what Fielden (2001) says as this provides an insight into Roman culture, the place of learning and Rome's overall decline and fall. On the status of private libraries, he says:

> "*There came a point that there were so many private libraries in Rome, that Seneca and Petronius both ridiculed the owners of these because the books were used as decorations instead of for their intended purpose. So much of this misuse was happening that some think*

> *that the famous line by Ammianus Marcellinus, "In short, the place of the philosopher the singer is called in, and in place of the orator the teacher of stagecraft, and while the libraries are shut up forever like tombs, water-organs are manufactured and lyres as large as carriages…"* refers to the total disuse of private libraries by the late 4th century because of the predominance of light entertainment over serious reading."[cxi]

On the Fringes

The 5th century marked a major decline in the fate of the Western Roman Empire as the Germanic peoples and tribes expanded into its territories. The Western Empire, after a long period of decline, was more vulnerable due to this Germanic migration and expansion, aided by their new rivals, the Eastern Roman Empire. Social relations in the countryside had altered rapidly as soldiers were rewarded land and, significantly, it is the *Pope* (Leo I) and his diplomacy who faced down adversaries in AD 450s rather than the might of the Emperor.

Being a Roman in Rome now offered little protection and provided no source of pride. However, like the Romans inheriting spoils of the Greek Empire, the invaders did not destroy Rome. These new settlers became Romanised, adopting the Latin language and utilising Roman institutions; elevating their own culture to help consolidate its rule. The Visigoths carried this adopted culture into Aquitaine and then into Hispania, the Iberian Peninsula.

Things were different in the Eastern Empire (Byzantium) where traditional Greco-Roman culture had remained intact. Greek was the official language and there was little use of Latin. [cxii].

However, on the periphery and outside of the direct influence of the Eastern Empire, three religions were influential in the Eastern regions - Zoroastrianism, Manicheism and, the new religion, Christianity. These were scripture-based religions and Christianity and Manicheism had also acquired Greek philosophical underpinnings. These factors indicated literacy and learning was strong within these communities and contributed to the Hellenisation of these regions.[cxiii]

At the heart of the Roman Empire, bitter, theological disputes took place to determine religious orthodoxy and establish Christian belief. These disputes resulted in the Nestorian Christians, who believed that God and Man existed within Jesus, leaving the Eastern Roman Empire in AD 462 and moving to Syria. They then relocated to Persia and were granted protection by the Sassanid Persian kings who were at constant war with Byzantium.

Theological centres, in places such as Nisibis, were set up and they created and used a curriculum that included use of Aristotelian logic within theological argument. This established a new route to the East through which classical texts were transported. Later, Nisibis also became a centre for the translation of texts from Greek to Syriac.[cxiv] The transfer of Greek culture and knowledge became more significant when it began to influence the Persian ruling class and intellectual life.[cxv] The ideas transported also contributed to the rise of Alchemy in the Middle East.

Most of the influential thinkers in late antiquity did not come from the heart of the Roman Empire but from its periphery, from areas such as Egypt, north-west Africa, Syria, Persia and Asia Minor.[cxvi]

Egypt, now a part of the Eastern Roman Empire, was a place where the grip of Constantinople had some limitations. The attempted imposition of a particular Christian orthodoxy did not work. Resistance by some, to key theological positions resulted in Egypt becoming a magnet for opposing Christian beliefs. One such group was the Coptic Christians who founded their church in Egypt.

Augustine of Hippo (354 – 430 CE), a Berber from North Africa (Algeria), is an example of an influential figure originating from the periphery of the Empire. His thinking and writing were to have a lasting influence, as his ideas allow some resolution between the many contradictory rationalist and mystical ideas of the time.

Following the traumatic sack of the Eternal City, Rome, by the Visigoths in AD 410, Augustine produced *The*

City of God against the Pagans (426 CE). Augustine's text refutes the arguments of those who believed Rome had been lost and abandoned by the gods due to the Christian suppression of Paganism and the closing of the temples. Augustine argued, to the contrary, it was the ineffective ancient gods who were unable to defend Rome. Salvation lay in the path of spiritually on earth.

Through his avid reading of philosophy, and his reflection on the many ideas of the time, he found his way through his contradictory thoughts. This

> *"...helped him to overcome his predisposition to materialism and paved the way for his...solution to the problem of evil, which enabled him to engage in the Neoplatonic ascent and thereby to overcome the fragmented isolation of bodies, the senses, and language."*[cxvii]

Using Aristotelian logic, Augustine said,

> *"True things cease to exist*
> *Truth is however eternal*
> *Truth must exist in something that is eternal"*

.... the immortal soul and the mind are aware of the unchanging truth and truths cannot be changed by the mind.

Empire Legacies

Many important texts were preserved within the East. With the Roman Empire now concentrated in Eastern

Byzantium, the struggle to maintain the Empire continued. Justinian (AD 482 – 565) heralded an era of civic renewal, including the significant initiative of consolidating all previous Roman law into a single system. He also decreed that teaching based only on the Christian faith was permitted, resulting in the school of Neoplatonic philosophy in Athens being repressed, and then abolished – although the school in Alexandria continued until the Arab conquest. For the next five centuries, philosophical teaching within the Byzantine Empire appears to have been limited to simple surveys of Aristotle's logic.[cxviii]

Over in Western Empire in Rome, now part of the Ostrogothic Kingdom, only Christian texts were translated.[cxix] Few people in the Western Roman Empire were interested in or prepared to preserve the old, pagan collections resulting in a diminishing of Roman culture. One exception to this was Roman senator and philosopher Boethius (c. 480-524/525), who translated Aristotle's works on logic from Greek into Latin - even if his motivation for doing this was a form of protest and standing up to the Eastern Empire.

Indicating how the embers of this knowledge might find a new location and champion, Fielden (2001) says,

> *"But, even at the end, on the western frontiers of the Empire, private libraries still existed and flourished and many became part of the monastic system that was to perpetuate writings during the medieval period."*[cxx]

Defining orthodoxies and heresies reflected the way that societies tried to clarify truth in the face of many competing ideas and challenges to authority. Alchemy, synthesising Greek natural philosophy, Platonism, artisanal experiment and an idea of the spirit and the divine, was one practice that faced repression by Roman rule. This repression will have resulted in alchemy becoming a shadowy and secret practice but also resulted in its dispersal to places far afield, along with its knowledge and ideas, influencing others more open to it.

CHAPTER FOUR

THE CITY OF PEACE and THE HOUSE OF WISDOM

WHEN and WHERE

AD 632 –1258

SAUDI ARABIA • SYRIA • IRAQ • SPAIN

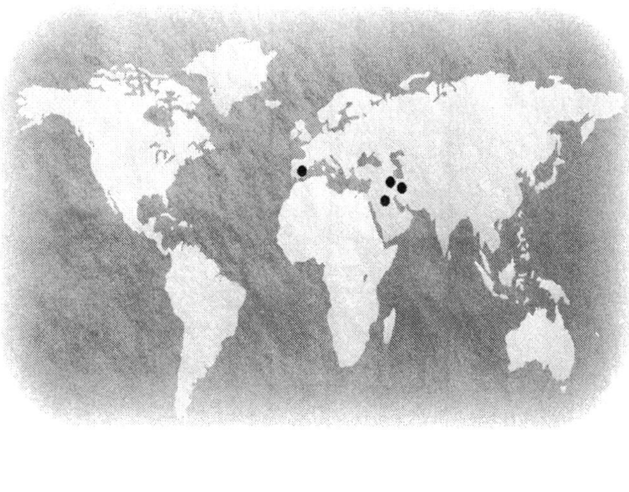

Getting your bearings

Between the 6th and 7th centuries AD, the old territories of the Western Roman Empire had been carved up by various armies and tribes from several different lands. As the fortunes of the Eastern Roman and Persian Empires (Sassanian) rose and fell, and the coffers of each ran dry, their territories were also threatened. From AD 630 onwards, tribes from the Arabian Peninsula, previously minor actors in the region, conquered lands from each of these old empires. They took parts of Spain in the West and, in the East, they took Syria and Egypt from the Byzantines and parts of Mesopotamia from the Persians. The rapid expansion of lands ruled by the Arabs gave rise to a new, Arabic civilisation, empire and religion, giving the quest for knowledge a new impetus.

Introduction

This chapter introduces the Arabic Empire and its relationship to alchemy. During the second Caliphate, when the Arabs conquered Egypt, influences from alchemy were incorporated and fused with both the practical industriousness and religious ideas of this new Arabic Civilisation. Alchemy became a mainstream activity within House of Wisdom.

Given the importance of the Arabic Empire for its collection, translation and use of ancient texts, this chapter primarily describes the way this was achieved. As our overall knowledge of this Empire tends to be less than that of the Western Empires, more detail is provided to help gain a fuller understanding of the contribution it made in the journey of knowledge and the search for Truth.

The chapter also describes some of the unique contributions made by Arabic civilisation, such as the methodological break made in natural philosophy. It also describes some of the advances made in the practical science, the incorporation of alchemy and the innovations made in mathematics. In addition the chapter looks at how the Arabs, like the Romans, fused ancient pagan philosophy with Abrahamic religion.

A New Religion

New conquerors emerged from the Arabian peninsula. The Arabs had their own emerging religion, Islam. Led by the Prophet Mohammed, who was from a prominent tribal trading family, Islam challenged the authority of the old, insular, tribal order that had been rooted in polytheism and aristocratic privilege. This coincided with those from the Arab peninsula developing a more united sense of a people. The new religion flowed out of a growing desire for a more spiritual religion, more akin to Judeo-Christian religions dominant across the region at the time. This desire for a spiritual shift can be seen in the adoption of an imported vocabulary of northern Syriac concepts like angels, devils, paradise and the practices of prayer and Bible story telling [cxxi].

Initially, Islam shared the Stoic and early Christian idea of an open community (citizens of the world) and was a potentially universal religion.[cxxii] Islam developed into a simple, monotheistic religion, with adherence to the rules and obligations of a practical life grounded in tradition, offering the prospect of an afterlife. It drew its authority from the record of revelations given to Mohammed from God which are passed on through the Qur'an and Hadith (the observations of the Prophet Muhammad).

The Caliphates

This section describes how each of the early Caliphates came about and their relationship to knowledge and learning. Alchemy is adopted as a discipline under the second and third Caliphates

The First Caliphate

After the death of the prophet Mohammed in AD 632, Abu Bakr (AD 573 – 634) was elected Caliph (successor), becoming Chief ruler of the first Caliphate (the Rashidun) established in Medina, north of Mecca. Bakr developed an army, drawn mostly from nomads who had few ties and were able to move rapidly across vast areas. Some of these recruits were also well-seasoned, experienced soldiers who had previously fought as part of either Byzantine or Persian military campaigns – and all were on the move. The pace of conquest was rapid, with Syria, Persia and Egypt all vanquished within twenty-five years.

However, from the outset of the Caliphate, tribal, religious and civil conflicts quickly surfaced resulting in civil wars between various sects with competing claims.

The Second Caliphate

The Umayyad dynasty, lasting from AD 661-750, arose from a leadership challenge by the Governor of Syria[cxxiii], Muawiyah (AD 602 – 661). The Umayyad's had been non-Muslims and their rule was more secular. Their victory also displaced the tradition of passing on leadership through tribal agreement to one based on a hereditary, family title and they shifted the centre of the Arab empire to Damascus[cxxiv].

They further extended the Empire, with invasions into India to the East, Carthage in North Africa and into Spain (the Iberian Peninsula) in the West. The Arabs retained influence over these vast geographical areas through large scale migration of Arabs into their conquered lands; allowing local elites of conquered lands to preserve their own institutions and bureaucracies; and by the Arabs retaining their own cultural distinctness by establishing garrison towns separate from conquered cities.[cxxv]

The Arabs forged a distinctive civilisation during this time through actions such as making Arabic the new language of administration and creating new coinage to impose their mark, helping to galvanize their authority.

The new Capital of Damascus was strategically very important. Firstly, it was near the numerous and lucrative trade routes in the region. They used their wealth to attract people from Byzantium into the new Capital, including those skilled in the vital crafts of state and administration. Muawiyah also adopted some of the outlook and sophisticated finery of the neighbouring Byzantine emperors, still resident in Constantinople.[cxxvi]

Recycling – professions, religion and alchemy

The new leaders left intact, rather than destroyed, much of what they inherited through conquest.[cxxvii] Many Christian and Jewish non-Arabs contributed to the emerging Arabic Empire, culture and civilisation, bringing with them various aspects of philosophical, legal, scholarly and cultural traditions.[cxxviii] Many aspects of these societies were absorbed and encouraged. Practically, they utilised the advanced knowledge available, such as pharmacology and metal, stone, and glass working, from places they had conquered, such as Egypt. Several documents show some of these fields were influenced by the tradition of Egyptian alchemy.[cxxix]

Whilst largely secular, Arabic courtly rule absorbed influences from the established Abrahamic faiths, shaping Islamic theological concepts such as free will, predestination, miracles, prophecy and the attributes of God[cxxx].

Beyond the Christian and Judaic faiths, there was also an interest in the more mystical, esoteric practices, again taken from Egypt, with its belief in the afterlife and divinity.

Two figures who illustrate how ideas were being assimilate are:

Khalid ibn Yazid (Calid) (AD 650 – 704). He was an Umayyad prince who collected books, facilitated translations of text into Arabic and is considered to provide a link between the Alexandrian and the subsequent Arabian schools of alchemy (al-Kimia)[cxxxi]. The practical knowledge of professions had a high status in the new Empire. Physicians, for example, developed a systematic approach to a study of drugs, their effects and antidotes. Religious belief and practical inquiry coexisted.

Jabir ibn Hayyan (Geber) (AD 721 – c. 815) lived between the second and third Caliphates. He is historically significant as he is considered the father of early chemistry; the first practical alchemist, experimenter, developer of laboratory equipment, crystallisation and distillation. However, Jabir did not seek to propagate his knowledge but

> *"...to baffle and lead into error everyone except those whom God loves and provides for."*[cxxxii]

His work was steeped in ancient thinking including Pythagorean and Neoplatonic systems[cxxxiii]. Like some Christians who practised theurgy, Jabir was interested in transformation and he saw experimentation as connected to divining the secrets and knowledge of life - the possibility of rearrangement of one substance in to another using some form of catalyst, known in Arabic as an *al-iksir*, to create the philosopher's stone.[cxxxiv]

The Third Caliphate

The Abbasids (from AD 750 – 1258) deposed the Umayyads, except for the territories within the Iberian Peninsula. The capital of the Arabic Empire and centre of the Caliphate was moved to Baghdad, chosen for its proximity to the old Persian city, Ctesiphon (southern Iraq).

Despite the significant challenges of maintaining power and control of this vast and varied empire, the Abbasids, just like the Umayyads had done, utilised the administration and personnel of another Empire, in this instance, from the imperial grandeur of the vanquished Persians. The Abbasids drew on the legacy of Persian scholarship and of translation, which had flourished under the patronage of the Emperor Chosroes I (aka Khosrow I). This provided one way to create a sense of continuity with the past, helping create some authority for the Caliphate to rule vast areas of territory from its relatively remote location[cxxxv].

They also utilised the treasure trove of culturally rich sources from across the empire and they absorbed and gave value to the scholarship, law and religion from areas such as those influenced by Hellenic and Roman culture.

For example, Christianity became established in Assyria (North Eastern Syria) from the first century AD. Then, in AD 431, Nestorian Christian priests moved to this region following a declaration of their heretical beliefs at the Council of Ephesus and the persecution they then faced as a result. And in AD 528, Persian King Chosroes I provided refuge to Greek Philosophers following the closure of the Platonic school in Athens by Justinian[cxxxvi]. Chosroes I let them settle in Ctestiphon, the ancient Persian Capital on banks of the Tigris, 35 KM South East of Baghdad, a Hellenistic City that had periodically been ruled by the Romans.

The House of Wisdom in The City of Peace

As well as absorbing influences, this new Arab Civilisation also made a mark, both contributing to and preserving scholarly and cultural developments inherited from other civilisations.

The early period of the Abbasid Caliphate shaped, what to become known as, the Islamic Golden Age, lasting in its entirety from the 8th to the 13th century. The three early Caliphs of this dynasty, Al-Mansur (AD 714 – AD 775), Harun al-Rashid (AD 763 - 809) and his son, al-Ma'mun (AD 786 –833), drew on ancient knowledge inherited from many sources. For instance, Al-Mansur, inspired by other Persian cities and the mathematician Euclid whom he had studied, used these architectural and mathematical influences in his construction of the circular city, Baghdad,[cxxxvii],[cxxxviii]. The City was known as Madinat al-Salaam or the '*City of Peace*'.

Similar confidence was shown by Al-Ma'mun who oversaw the creation of **The House of Wisdom** (*Bayt al-Hikma*). This was, most probably, an archival store and it gave rise to authorised scholastic activity contributing to the emergence of the Islamic Golden Age[cxxxix]. The activity of amassing a vast collection of ancient texts takes place during al-Ma'mun's rule and the flourishing of ideas is aided through this process.[cxl] This enterprise was subsidised by an enormous outlay of funds, both public and private. Hoyland (2014) thinks that some of the impetus driving Arab learning was its use as an intellectual weapon in a culture war conducted against the old empires, and a way to gain further prestige and influence.[cxli]

Whilst much of this activity took place within the court of the Caliphates, some wealthy families also hosted Salons which became a key focus of intellectual life; a more informal setting where ideas could emerge[cxlii].

One core aspect of the Islamic Golden Age was the Great Translation Movement, led by Al Kindi (AD 801 - 873), from Basra, Iraq. The Translation Movement was aided by newly acquired knowledge of paper production, taken from the East, and of book binding and book creation [cxliii]. As a centre for translation, copying and book binding, the House of Wisdom was no passing whim. It was supported by caliphs and princes, civil servants and military leaders, merchants and bankers along with scholars and scientists[cxliv] and lasted for a couple of hundred years.

Gutas (1998) argues that the passion for translation went far beyond the preserve of the elite. Interest in ancient works, which the Abbasids had made central to society, was shared much more broadly in society with others commissioning translations to further their, mostly, practical inquiry.[cxlv] And,

> *"....it was eventually conducted with rigorous scholarly methodology and strict philological exactitude— by the famous Hunayn ibn-Ishaq and his associates — on the basis of a sustained program that spanned generations and which reflects, in the final analysis, a social attitude and the public culture of early 'Abbasid society."*[cxlvi]

Gutas (1998) argues that it was the culture that drove the demand for translation,

> *"It was the development of an Arabic scientific and philosophical tradition that generated the*

> *wholesale demand for translations from the Greek (and Syriac and Pahlavi), not, as is commonly assumed, the translations which gave rise to science and philosophy).”*[cxlvii]

Many of these texts were translated into Arabic by, predominantly, Christians and Jews from the territories to the north of Baghdad.[cxlviii] Two early translations were texts by Aristotle. The *Topics* and *The Physics* were translated in the AD 780s. His *Metaphysics* was not being translated until early in the 9th century. These early translations were pivotal in establishing the use of logic in the development of competing religious ideas[cxlix].

However, translations were often made using texts that were interpretations of ancient Greek Philosophers and which had several consequences. A work by the Egyptian, Plotinus, *The Enneads*, is one such example. It was written in the 3rd century AD, it had been inspired by Plato’s *Timaeus* and then edited and arranged systematically by Porphyry.

Uzdavinys (2009) says,

> *“Plotinus exercised his influence on the Islamic world under the mask of Aristotle, and the Arabic version of the Enneads paradoxically became known as the Theology of Aristotle.”*[cl]

Practical inquiry and experience provided a strong impetus to the Translation Movement. Euclid, Galen, Pythagoras, Hippocrates and Aristotle[cli] were considered important for their mathematics, astronomy, medicine, optics, alchemy and chemistry, zoology, geography and cartography. These were then followed by new Arabic innovations in areas such as algebra, numerals and chemical experimentation. The scholars from the House of Wisdom often doubled as engineers and architects in major construction projects, keeping accurate official calendars, acting as public servants and becoming medics and consultants.[clii]

This range of knowledge and scholarship produced Arabic polymath, Al-Razi (Rhazes, AD 854 – 925, Waqas Rey, near Tehran, Iran/Persia). He worked within this new culture of logic and reasoning. He was a doctor, serving as the Chief Physician of Baghdad. He was also a philosopher, a scholar, a chemist and - an alchemist. An early proponent of experimental medicine, he was typical of many scholars working across disciplines and he was known for his numerous observations and discoveries[cliii]. Al-Razi also believed these many disciplines were intimately connected through religion. Ibn Al-Nadim, a 10th-century scholar, provided his view on Al-Razi's beliefs,

> *"...the study of philosophy could not be considered complete, and a learned man could not be called a philosopher, until he has succeeded in producing the alchemical transmutation."*[cliv]

In an important advance in methodology that was to have significant consequences over time, Al-Razi's curiosity and use of empirical methods and logical speculation resulted in a separation between inquiry from archaic formulas and numerology. Significantly, this severed the need to understand physical processes from knowledge of the divine will – which, in time, allowed the discipline of chemistry to emerge.

His works contain detailed descriptions of methodology and the equipment used during experiments. He wrote several treatises, the most important of which became known as *Liber Secretorum Bubacaris* (The Book of Secrets of Secrets). It contained the details of many practical recipes and processes, such as distillation and crystallisation, and became known to Western Science and was regarded for centuries as an important foundational work.[clv]

Philosophy and Religion

During the Abbasid Caliphate, theological and philosophical ideas developed. This section illustrates the intimate connection and influence Greek philosophical thinking had on Islam's development; an area likely to be unfamiliar to many. It also describes the fusing of ideas with Arabic advances in practical experiment, influential in the ongoing evolution of alchemy and its adoption in later periods.

The development of ideas within the period of the third Caliphate was shaped by, and a reaction to, other dominant belief systems. As with the Roman Christians before them, theological clarity against other religions was needed in order to assert the superiority of Islam.

Some Arabic theologians, the *traditionalists*, took scripture literally, seeing it as the actual word of god. And their God had an 'awful will', to which everyone must submit himself without question.

'*Rationalists*', on the other hand, pursued philosophy (falsafa) or theology (kalam), using concepts and ideas drawn from other traditions. The Muʿtazilah were

> "*...the first Muslims to use the categories and methods of Hellenistic philosophy to derive their three major and distinctive theological dogmatic points*"[clvi].

In contrast to traditionalists, they used logical reasoning and concepts drawn from Greek philosophy, such as from Plotinus's 'The one' and the Pythagorean concept of a trapped soul in the body.

Theological dispute resulted in internal conflicts and, importantly, the rationalist position was proclaimed to be state dogma by Caliph al-Maʾmūn in AD 827. However, a powerful class of religious scholars (the Ulama), disagreed[clvii], asserting the *traditionalist* view. Ultimately, the aim of the Caliph to impose a rationalist interpretation of the Muslim faith through the 'Minha', a form of early inquisition, failed. The traditionalist view of religious scholars prevailed, weakening both the absolute authority of the Caliph and of rationalist thought. However, within this broad trend, a few key people carried forward the rationalist tradition.

Al-Kindi (AD 801 - 873) developed an Arabic philosophical vocabulary through which philosophical concepts could be debated and through which he began to fashion a 'rationalist' religion for intellectuals.

Al-Farabi (AD 872 – c.951) was the first Arabic philosopher who attempted to develop a single *universal* system within which conflicting ideas could be explained and reconciled. He was also influenced by utopian Platonic ideas, developing his own concept of the ideal city. He believed his philosophy, known as Falsafa, was superior to other types of knowledge, as it provided the possibility of *universal* knowledge compared to other systems that could provide only *particular* knowledge [clviii]

one of the most significant Arabic scholars, Ibn-Sina (AD 980 – 1037 aka Avicenna), lived at a time when central control of Baghdad had waned. This meant, like many scholars of his day, he was compelled to live an itinerant life, seeking patronage from Court to Court - travelling from his home in Bukhara, Uzbekistan down through Turkmenistan and into Iran (a distance of some 2,000 miles as the crow flies).

Whilst medicine was one of his specialist areas, and his work was later to provide the standard medical texts for universities until as late as 1650s, he also strove, like Al-Farabi, to develop a systematic philosophical method that would provide a coherent and compelling rationalist explanation of truth.

To achieve this, he first drew together and ordered his sources, including ideas from Greek philosophy, including Aristotle; taking over eighteen years to complete this task[clix]. Ibn-Sina developed a theory of knowledge that went beyond the idea of revelation from scripture or the use of pure logic.

One idea taken from Aristotle, which was to become hugely influential on the philosopher John Locke, was the view that,

> *"The human rational soul, upon its first creation, is absolutely potential, a tabula rasa."*[clx]

Ibn-Sina argued that logic was insufficient for gaining knowledge. He believed that familiarity with the world was needed. Although God may have been the First Cause, it is only man, not God, who experiences the earthly manifestations of God's initial work.

Ibn-Sina adopted Aristotle's curriculum and logical methods. He made the case that before arriving at higher forms of truth, such as the principles of geometry (*universal truth*), or of language or specific religions (*particular truth*), empirical familiarity and the use of the 'active intellect' was needed.[clxi]

He also applied his system to find proof of the existence of God.

One of the most influential thinkers in the development of Islam, Al-Ghazali (AD 1058 – 1111) from Tous, Iran/Persia, was a philosopher, theologian and jurist, unlike Al-Kindi, Al-Razi, Ibn-Sina and Ibn-Rushd who were Polymaths immersed in both philosophy and practical life and experimentation. Al-Ghazali was a rationalist but, through his own systematic study of the rationalist method, he challenged what he deduced were the flawed arguments in key ideas within Falsafa. He disagreed on free will, for example, [clxii], and he reasserted Islamic belief in a created world, the resurrection of the body, and God's knowledge of the particular, and the future.[clxiii] Amongst those he influenced were the Almohad Caliphate (Northern Africa Berbers and whose rule extended into the Iberian Peninsula) and later, Western medieval thinkers such as Thomas Aquinas.

Spain's Difference

Arabic philosophers in Muslim Al-Andalus (in the Iberian peninsula), the most western part of the Arab Empire, had a different relationship to Islam providing an alternative strand within the development of Arabic and Islamic ideas. This region started to become prominent from AD 756 when the Umayyad prince, Abd-al-Rahman I from Damascus, escaped the Abbasid massacre of his family in Syria and established himself in Córdoba.[clxiv]

With its distance from the dominant religious ideology of the Abbasid dynasty based in Baghdad, the Arab rulers of the southern strongholds of the Empire were influenced by ideas coming from different sources - the North African Berber tribes, who they were militarily dependent on, the firmly established Judeo/Christian tradition and some more practical scholarships that focused on mathematics, astronomy and medicine. Arabic philosophy from the East only began to be influential in this region once the early translation work from the House of Wisdom was completed and their influence had moved Westwards.[clxv]

It was under Abd al-Rahman II (AD 792 – 852) and Al-Hakam II (AD 915 – 976) that scholarship really began to flourish in this region. Al-Hakam became known as the patron of knowledge and he provided financial incentives to scholars to help make Córdoba the centre of learning. Free from the more fundamentalist Islamic control, Córdoba outpaced Baghdad as the centre of learning - and its success can be seen when it became attractive to scholars from the East. Al-Andalus also provided a key route through which ancient texts found their way back to the West.

Maslama al-Majriti (c AD 950 - 1007), was from Madrid, in the centre of the Iberian Peninsula and is an example of a polymath working within the Arabic west during this period. He was considered the foremost authority on astronomy by his contemporaries.[clxvi] He was also a geographer, economist and, significantly, a chemist. He established a school for systematic research, arithmetic and geometry, providing much groundwork for scientific developments that would take place in the 18th and 19th centuries. He both improved and translated texts.

Libraries were established across the Muslim areas of the peninsula. Al-Hakam's Córdoban library was said to have employed 500 staff and its books were gathered from both the Arab and Byzantine Empires[clxvii]. He created a translation committee of Muslim and Christian scholars. He also created a large book market providing one of the few great public civic institutions through which learning could be acquired. This resulted in a significant rise in literacy, far outstripping that within Europe of the time.

Indicative of the advance thinking of rationalist ideas in Spain was their suspicion of some of the new ideas being generated by scholars of the Abbasid court in the East. Western scholars thought their Eastern counterparts provided inadequate distinctions between the sciences and pseudo-sciences. Even Ibn Hazm, a leading but staunchly conservative Andalusian scholar of the 11th century, was very outspoken on this point, calling those advocating the efficacy of talismans, magic, alchemy and astrology, shameless liars. This rational approach in the West resulted in Islam's pre-eminence within the natural sciences[clxviii]. And, as a fitting testament to the success of Al-Hakam's patronage, books by scholars, even by those still residing within the Abbasid kingdom, were dedicated to him.

Challenges East to West

By the 11th century, external and internal threats to the Islamic world were closing in. In the East, between AD 1095 and 1099, the Byzantine Empire conducted its first crusade into the Holy Land, retaking Jerusalem. And in the West, the Christians continued to threaten a reconquest of the Iberian Peninsula.

In the West, control of the Caliphate of Córdoba had crumbed within sixty years of Al-Hakam's death, leaving divided territories under the Taifa kings from AD 1031. These rulers were reliant on military support from Moroccan Berbers who exerted a more conservative, traditionalist and intolerant influence on a culture where coexistence between religions had been strong. Ironically, in the short term, fragmentation also allowed space for new ideas to develop.

Some prominent scholars who honed their ideas during this time were Ibn Rushd (aka Averroes, AD 1126 – 1198) and Ibn Tufail (c. AD 1105 – 1185). Both were physicians at the Court of Almohad Sultan, and they had benefitted from the scholarship and texts that had been brought from the East.

Ibn Tufail wrote the first philosophical novel *Hayy ibn Yaqdhan* (*The Living Son of the Vigilant* or "*Alive, Son of Awake*") which was to prove very influential on the thinking of philosopher John Locke 500 years later.

Tufail's novel is a thought experiment, around the concept of Tabula Rasa (blank slate). This concept was originally developed by Aristotle and then by Ibn Sina (Avicenna). In this story, it is assumed that people learn through their experience and they are born with no existing (a *priori*) knowledge. Tufail's novel unfolds using symbolism and religious allegory depicted through the books main character, the baby Hayy. Hayy is washed up on a deserted island and brought up by a gazelle. Following the death of the loving creature that had cared for him, Hayy begins to learn through his experiences. For example, he becomes self-aware by comparing himself to the other creatures he encounters. He also observes the actions of a community of people living on a nearby island and, from this, he concluded that he prefers solitude and quiet contemplation. Ultimately, he discovers a mystic union and enlightenment.

Another prominent figure is the Jewish Córdoban scholar, philosopher and physician, Maimonides (AD 1135– 1204) who was influenced by Jewish and Islamic legal jurisprudence (Fiqh) and law. Maimonides, a contemporary to various scholastic debates happening in other parts of Europe, contributed to this wider discussion by trying to achieve a viewpoint that balanced philosophy, science and religion.

Based on the descriptions above, the contribution the Arabs made to practical knowledge seems uncontroversial, and their cultural achievement in the translation of ideas, spurring on intellectual thinking is hugely significant. However, there is more contention on their contribution to the development of new ideas.

Malik (2011) argues that the portrayal of the Islamic world as comprising of only rationalist or traditionalist interpretations of Islam overlooks the many free thinkers and religious sceptics that also existed. For example, Al-Razi and Al-Ma'arri were often criticised, or even considered heretics (dubbed Zindiqs[clxix]).

Russell (1946) contends that the period during the ascendency of the Arab Empire saw little by way of new contributions to philosophy [clxx], arguing that for five centuries, much philosophical teaching was limited to simple surveys of Aristotle's logic.[clxxi]

Some contemporary academics, such as Adamson and Gutas, argue the contribution of the Arabs to philosophy was more significant.[clxxii]

However, it is without doubt that Arabic civilisation took study and scholarship very seriously. Their melding of theological and philosophical ideas, the break they made in methodological approach and their advances in practical experiment were significant and proved to be very influential in the development of alchemy and the scientific method of the future. Their preservation of knowledge also ensured that some of the most significant ideas from the past were saved for future generations.

CHAPTER FIVE

THE GENERAL HOUSE of STUDIES

WHEN and WHERE

AD 800 -1250

AACHEN • HEREFORD • TOLEDO • PARIS • COLOGNE

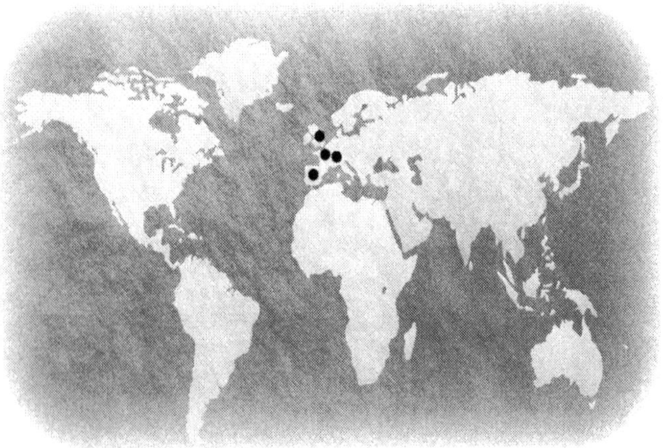

Getting your bearings

With the Western Roman Empire falling to a Germanic prince in AD 476, there followed a period of cultural decline within the territories of the old Western Roman Empire. During this period, the western regions were roughly divided between three empires – the Carolingian, Arab and Byzantine Empires. The next few hundred years were tumultuous, with a gradual shift of axis towards Northern Europe. This change was initially spurred on through the creation of a new Empire under Charlemagne in the 8th century and by Papal ambitions.

Importantly, during this period, the Caliphate of Córdoba lost its control (1031), the Byzantine Empire lost territory to the Turks and the Holy Lands, including Jerusalem, that had been lost to the Arabs in the 7th Century, were reconquered during The First Crusade (1095–1099). Significant tensions emerged between the Catholic Church and strengthening secular forces. In the 1300s the Church also faced internal challenges from scholars, such as the Englishman John Wycliffe and Czech theologian Jan Hus, who questioned both the role of the Church and some of its fundamental teachings.

Introduction

Alchemy plays a small but important part in this chapter, with alchemical texts being introduced to the West around the 1200s AD. This chapter mainly pieces together *why* the transportation of knowledge into different parts of Europe took place during this time – and alchemy made up just one part of this cargo. This is important for setting the scene for why and how alchemy moves to a much more prominent position described in future chapters.

The chapter provides a broad description of some of the consequences of the rise and fall of civilisations and explores the reaction of the Catholic Church as it began to lose its authority to secular power. It considers the tensions lying at the heart of the acquisition of ancient knowledge and in the demand for manuscripts from antiquity and from various empires and kingdoms. Some classical knowledge had been retained in small pockets within Europe, such as within Ireland, but knowledge was also imported through a number of different routes.

Rebooting Knowledge in the West

The rise of Charlemagne (AD 742 – 814) and his new Carolingian Christian empire created a new demand for learning. Charlemagne made scholarship a centre-piece of his court in Aachen, Germany. He imported knowledge, as the Caliphates and others had done before him and he attracted several scholars with the aims of improving his administration and establishing Latin as the common language throughout his empire. Aiding this mission, he supported the introduction of the classical liberal arts curriculum[clxxiii], using scholars as priests and scribes. One of these was the great Greek-speaking Irish scholar, Scotus/Erugina. However, following Charlemagne's death, his Empire had fragmented by AD 1100, partly due to a reversion to an old tradition of dividing succession between sons.

King Knut/Canute (AD 990 – 1035) provides another example of someone using knowledge to aid his consolidation of power and authority. After conquering England, he brought his own churchmen to England to replace the Anglo-Saxon monks whom he didn't trust. Surprisingly we find that, at this time, Hereford was a centre of Arabic studies and Robert de Losinga and French abbot Guibert de Nogent (who later penned a tribute to the value of Arabic astronomy[clxxiv]) were based there serving the Danish king.

Spiritual Knowledge and Certainty – and a Horseload of Books

Around this same time, in the 990s, the Roman-based church was grappling with deep-rooted tensions that had emerged between spiritual and temporal institutions within the West; between the rule of church and the rule of kings and princes. The Church needed new means by which they could end such challenges and through which they would become the undisputed arbiters of truth, with God-given authority to be so. The most important factor driving a transfer of knowledge into the heart of Europe was that the Roman Church and the Papacy thought they might identify new sources of evidence from which they could re-assert the legitimacy of their power.

A further, and not insignificant factor in the new movement of knowledge, was the growing awareness in parts of Europe that the Arabic Civilisation was far in advance of any in Europe. There was a desire to gain a better understanding of, for example, Arabic advances in science and astrology. To catch up, Arabic works of applied and practical science and knowledge of the cosmos and astrology were needed.

It should be remembered that circa AD 1,000, some of the major cities under Arab rule such as Córdoba, Constantinople, Alexandria and Palermo, each had upwards of 350,000 people with Baghdad having a population of around 1.2m. In Northern Europe, most large towns, such as Paris, London and Cologne, only numbered about 20,000 people[clxxv], [clxxvi].

With levels of literacy and education virtually non-existent in Europe, other than amongst the clergy, and an evident disparity in levels of knowledge, many were keen to bridge this gap.[clxxvii] Scholars, such as Adelard of Bath (AD 1080 – 1152), travelled to Spain and Sicily, translating works on astronomy and mathematics, including the first complete translation of Euclid's *Elements* into Latin.[clxxviii]

One of the earliest episodes of Arabic sciences being transported out of Spain and northward across the Alps occurred in AD 953. John of Gorze had been dispatched to Córdoba on a diplomatic mission from the Holy Roman Emperor, Otto the Great. He ended up staying in Spain, becoming the Caliph's physician for three years. However, when he finally returned, he did so with "a horseload" of Arabic books.[clxxix] And later, Arnold of Villanova (AD 1235, Valencia) is credited with translating a number of medical texts from Arabic, including works by Ibn-Sina (Avicenna), Abu-al-Salt and Galen.

Another way Church activity overcame the cultural gap was through encouraging the flourishing of the Scholastic method. This originated in the many autonomous monasteries and cathedral schools across Europe. The Duke of Aquitaine, for example, founded the Cluniac Order in AD 910 (the Order that established the School of Translation in Toledo). Teachings within such orders were generally based around the seven liberal arts. Some used the trivium (logic, grammar and rhetoric), which aided the rigorous application of the dialectical method, along with the practice of disputation and use of logic. Some schools, like the School of Chartres, used the quadrivium (arithmetic, geometry, music and astronomy), along with the study of Plato's *Timaeus*, a speculation on the nature of the physical world and human beings.[clxxx]

Unusually, the Duke of Aquitaine, created a different form of patronage, making his Order answerable to the Papacy rather than to himself[clxxxi]. This meant that resolving contradictions evident in scripture and writings, and using logic to demonstrate the authority of scripture, acquired a strongly instrumental purpose under the direction of the Church. This was important given subsequent developments.

One significant move by the Roman Church in the mid-11th century was its effort to establish its preeminent authority through the initiation of the Gregorian Reforms (AD 1050 – 1080). It used Canon Law to establish hierarchical authority over secular power[clxxxii]. Scripture, as a source of authority, created further demand for Latin translations and interpretations of manuscripts and, based on these, heretical views clarified.

Scholasticism, a discipline utilising classical logic and methodology contributed to this process.

Gathering texts

To achieve this goal, *The Schoolmen* required classical texts. Identifying and collecting ancient text became an important activity over the next couple of hundred years. The following sections show the diverse sources from where these texts came from, moving forward the journey of knowledge.

Latin Texts

Initially, the material available for this project was minimal as only a few Latin translated works by the ancients were available. For example, there were the Latin translations of Aristotle by Boethius and an encyclopaedia (*Etymologies*) that had attempted to encompass all Classical Greek and Roman knowledge compiled by St Isidore of Seville (c.AD 560-636)[clxxxiii]. There was also the work of John Scotus Eriugena (AD c. 815 – c. 877), the Irish Neo-Platonist theologian, who translated pseudo-Dionysius from Greek to Latin.

Arabic Texts

The monastery of Ripoll (in the eastern Pyrenees), established in the mid-10th, was the site of the first attempts in the West to synthesize the "Arabo-Greek corpus" in Latin.

Access to texts in Arabic mainly occurred as a result of the Christian reconquest of cities and territories within the Iberian Peninsula and other areas previously held by the Arabs. The first of such conquests was the capture of Toledo in AD 1085 by Alfonso VI of Castile and his Christian forces. From around AD 1120, a new translation movement emerged, but this time sponsored from within Europe.

As mentioned above, the Cluniac order established the Toledo School of Translators. This was followed by a second school in Palermo, Sicily. The School at Toledo was led by Archbishop Raymond de Sauvetât (AD 1125 - 1152). It translated Arabic and other texts into Latin, a task undertaken mainly by translators from England. The group recovered ancient and more contemporary texts which aided major advances at the Toledo School of Medicine and for others in the areas of algebra and astronomy[clxxxiv] Slightly later, came translations of astronomical, mathematical, medical and philosophical works of scientists working during the medieval period in the East.[clxxxv] Under King Alfonso X of Castile (AD 1252–1284), the translators no longer worked with Latin as the final language, but rather translated texts into a revised version of Castilian, which helped form a unified language across the Peninsula.

Greek Texts

A key source of Greek texts was via Constantinople, the Greek-speaking centre of the Byzantine Empire.

There had been quite a plentiful supply of these texts as, from the 9th century onwards, the Byzantines had dramatically increased the number they copied. Gutas

(1998) explores both the reasons for the increase in copied texts (possibly a reaction to the cultural level of the Arabs and a recognition of the Byzantine's neglect of scholarship) *and* the type of texts translated compared to those translated within the Arab Empire (the Byzantine's giving more focus to humanistic rather than technical / scientific texts)[clxxxvi].

AD 1054 had brought the 'Great Schism' between the Roman and Greek Churches. The Roman Church attempted to assert its universal authority over the Greek Church, as the latter was seen as being more subservient to the Holy Roman Emperor[clxxxvii]. A major break came with the Latin Christian Fourth Crusade (1202–04) and the sacking of Constantinople in 1204. This was a shocking event, being an assault by Christian upon Christian. However, one product of this attack, was the breaking open of a reservoir of writings, such as classical texts by Aristotle, many in the original Greek, becoming available for the first time to those outside of the Byzantine Empire.

The sections above, on Latin, Arabic and Greek texts, describe the many routes and sources from which classical text entered the wider regions of Europe. These texts included neo-Platonic metaphysics, cosmology and some Aristotle, providing logic and intellectual categories[clxxxviii]. These provided the raw material (incorporating dialectical method, logic, grammar) for the detailed examination of scripture and disputation of meaning that was being undertaken.

The purpose behind these endeavours was mainly to create more compelling Christian arguments[clxxxix]. This scholarship created further demand, creating the impetus for importing even more ancient ideas. By the 1250s, the whole of Aristotle's work was available as a single corpus. Burnett (2001) argues that it was the cathedral schools, and the emerging universities, that created the high demand for the Latin translation undertaken in Toledo. It was the demand for the texts, not just their availability, that resulted in this movement of ideas.[cxc]

The study of theology was controlled by the Church and it was only taught in a relatively few universities, such as Paris, Oxford, Cambridge and Rome, growing out of older Cathedral schools. To provide the rigour necessary for gaining greater spiritual understanding, Scholasticism drew on a wide range of knowledge from religious scripture, but also from pagan philosophy. The *Schoolmen* then applied logic, dialectics and disputation to resolve contradictory ideas and to arrive at a solid truth, affirm the authority of the Church and provide a clear testament against heresy and magic.

New universities, emerging in Italy and other parts of Europe, created a new dynamic around the study of a wider range of disciplines focused on the liberal arts curriculum. The teaching of the arts then also extended to the more traditional cathedral schools.

Taught in the arts faculty, the new translations of Aristotle that had become available transformed learning, creating a limited yet important space for thinking to develop. This space afforded a degree of freedom from the strictures of the scholastic tradition and from the Church.[cxci] A re-examination of logic, universals, eternity, causality and mathematical reasoning fostered a separation between scholarly disciplines.

It is a profound irony that, given the Church had instigated this level of inquiry, the expansion of study brought a loosening rather than a strengthening, of religious control. Conventional doctrine was generally adhered to, but, understanding how knowledge and the truth were acquired created an abundance of new ways of thinking [cxcii]

Making Sense – Observation, Sense Perception, Language and Creativity

Albertus Magnus /Albert the Great (AD 1206 – 1280), saw that natural philosophy, the unique human intellect for observation, experiment and the application of reason were all important for gaining an enriched understanding of the world.

He was the most influential in emphasising that natural philosophy is a self-sufficient discipline, different from theology which seeks to understand only the natural world. Therefore, it should only be concerned with sensory evidence and logical demonstration.[cxciii] Albert assimilated ideas from various sources, including Arabic and Neoplatonic writing and a clear link on his thinking about the separateness of natural philosophy as a discipline might be traced back to Al-Razi (Rhazes, AD 854 – 925) who held a similar view.

Albert was sent by the Church to Cologne in Germany to organise the first Dominican *Studium Generale* (**The General House of Studies**). This new monastic order of the Dominicans worked in urban centres, such as Paris[cxciv], and

> *"...devoted themselves to the elaboration of an entire philosophical system erected on the twin foundations of Greek and Christian thought.*[cxcv]

A student of Albert, fellow Dominican Thomas Aquinas (AD 1225–1274), believed sense perception and faith were necessary to understand Truth. Studying in Naples, Paris and Cologne, he was one of the first in Northern Europe during this period to read the whole of Aristotle's work. From this, he judged that sense perception was necessary for gaining an understanding of the world, where the cause of things can be established through observed effects.

His conclusions are set out in his *Summa Theologica* (written 1265–1274); "caused" things "are never quite the same as their cause and this applies to the relationship between creation and Creator. Like the Sun's distribution of heat throughout the earth, God's attributes are distributed throughout his creation in a limited way."[cxcvi] Or, according to 1 Corinthians 13:12. Geneva Bible 1560

> *"For now we see through a glass darkly; but then face to face: now I know in part;*
> *but then shall I know even as also I am known."*

Roger Bacon (c. AD 1214–1294), a Franciscan friar, was rigorous in his study using his knowledge of languages and science to gain a better understanding of theology in the service of Christendom (the *Res Publica Christiana*).[cxcvii] He became critical of religious scholarship when he discovered errors in some of the translated scriptures. He learnt even more languages so that he could study original sources and produce new, grammatically accurate copies, which he could also translate into other languages. He also thought it woeful that scholars were prepared to accept the authority of the church on any matter rather than using their own judgement based on science. The meaning of science at this time was derived from Aristotle in that it,

> *"...denotes intellectual comprehension of a true, necessary, and universal proposition, known or presented in the form of a demonstrative proof and providing an understanding of why the proposition is true. In other words, Aristotelian science involves knowledge of a reasoned fact - an understanding of science that is far broader than the modern understanding of empirical science."*[cxcviii]

As a correction to the weaknesses he had identified, he made the case for radical changes to the medieval university curriculum, arguing that new disciplines, such as perspective (optics), experimental science, alchemy, and mathematics, were perhaps necessary for establishing truth.[cxcix]

Ramon Llull (AD 1232 Majorca) was influential in using logic and science to try to further the Christian cause. He too was influenced by Aristotle and natural science, although he had a more mechanical view of facts and knowledge. He believed that the truths about a field of knowledge could be established by studying any combination of elemental truths. In an inspired leap of imagination, he then thought that these could then be turned into fixed lists, which could be mechanically generated, and then used to demonstrate the truth to others.[cc]

Paul of Taranto (AD 1250), a Franciscan alchemist from Southern Italy, developed his ideas around the uniqueness of the human intellect compared to other animals.

He looked at how different activities utilised the intellect to change the substance of things. This might be done superficially, such as the way a sculptor changes material to create a new form. He compares that activity with, for example, the actions of physicians or farmers who are involved in perfective activity, using the elements (earth, fire, water, air) to change the primary qualities of substances.

More Answers, More Questions

As the descriptions above demonstrate, having been instrumental in introducing this multiplicity of ideas in their attempts to establish 'Truth', and thereby the authority of the Church, scholars of the 13th and early 14th centuries had instead identified or created multiple, and often contradictory viewpoints.

Olsen (1982) identifies the contrasting positions scholars adopted when attempting to resolve conflicting statements that emerged from different sources and methods of study.

Commonly, many gave primacy to theological principles above philosophical ones. Others said that there are different kinds of truth or that where there is a conflict, the philosophical statement must be accepted as true. Finally, there was the position of Aquinas, the position ultimately adopted by the Church - conflict occurred only due to misinterpretation. He argued that there should be acceptance of distinct goals; that experience of the natural world is an essential part of learning; however, the higher goal is to transcend this. [cci]

The Church had created a path littered with unintended consequences and it now needed to manage the fallout of this.

New Heresies and Witches

The problem was further exacerbated by the fact that the teaching provided within the Arts Faculties was no longer taught just by the churchmen who regarded themselves as arbiters of the Truth. Despite, or because of, this expansion of those who could teach, Dominicans were enlisted to help define heresy and the lines that could not be crossed. This was then tested in the City of Paris. From AD 1210 – 1277, lists of heretical teachings, known as the Paris Condemnations, were drawn up. *Prohibited* teachings included specific articles such as: 'The World is Eternal'; 'There Was Never a First Human'; or 'Human Acts Are Not Governed by The Providence of God'. Furthermore, some texts were banned including texts of Aristotle's natural philosophy.

Despite significant effort, the Church was still finding it hard to assert its authority and it experimented with new ways to do this. At this time, the foundations of law (Roman, Canon and Feudal law) and complex administration and bureaucracy, were built into the workings of society; reaching down into the minutiae of the day to day lives of citizens. The Church began to intensify its pastoral efforts, instructing the laity in proper belief, reinforcing the practice of annual confession. They found ways to observe what was going on throughout society and where and how heretical views were being practised. They then defined new heresies in response to what they saw. [ccii] The Dominicans, including Aquinas, were then enlisted into roles aimed at neutralising and stamping out the spreading of these created heresies using new inquisitorial procedures and judicial torture adopted from Roman Law [cciii].

Ironically, with people such as Aquinas and William of Auvergne, the Bishop of Paris, exploring all manner of texts and ideas, they had also created the foundation for a new interest in magic through their elaboration of how it worked. For example, explanations had been set out on how demons operated at the behest of magicians within the natural laws of, an essentially, Aristotelian universe. [cciv]

Furthermore, through Aquinas's work '*Summa contra Gentiles*' (AD 1259 - 1265), the Church now identified *maleficium* (sorcery) with heresy. Prior to this, witchcraft was viewed as an old pagan ritual that was tried through secular courts. The evil of the devil, tricking gullible sorcerers to act against God, was transformed into the act of an evil person; a devil worshiper. The significant rise of witchcraft trials began after this turning point.[ccv] Their elaboration of ancient occult practices may also have generated an interest in magic…but also manufactured a new source of evil, resulting in persecution over the next couple of centuries [ccvi]

Despite the many efforts of The Church to limit the interest in ancient philosophy, by AD 1270 the appeal of Aristotle was proving to be too strong and the Condemnations lost their force. Furthermore, seen from our historical vantage point, the Church had unwittingly propelled forward the development of modern scientific thinking. In their effort to establish a definitive truth, using logic to create new definitions of heresy, aided by Aquinas, rationalist thinking became widespread.[ccvii]

One such paradoxical outcome arose from the argument, put forward by the theologian-philosopher William of Ockham (AD 1285 – 1347). He questioned that there was any relationship between natural philosophy and theology and argued for their total separation, as scientific enquiry could only ever be contingent. And as Man only had mortal existence, he also had a limited ability to demonstrate any knowledge of the essence of God. The logic of this was a freeing of scientific inquiry from any obligation to resolve contradictions in cause and revelation; allowing disciplines such as mathematics to develop unhindered.[ccviii] Ockham's belief in the limitations of empiricism, and of cause and effect, laid the basis for a separation between philosophy and theology – and the potential for theoretic sciences. As Olsen (1982) explains:

> *"...he denied that any first principles could have empirical content, since all experience is contingent rather than necessary. This means that all true sciences had to be about nothing more than the concepts that the terms of the propositions signified."*[ccix]

Boosting the authority of those with power through the acquisition of knowledge had occurred in previous eras. However, the consequences of the Church-driven scholarship during this period had unintended consequences that were to reverberate for centuries.

The imperative of finding, translating and using new knowledge had opened a Pandora's Box. Alchemy only makes up one small part of the new wealth of knowledge that began to become available in the West.

However, overall, this new body of knowledge resulted in different ways of thinking, proving virtually impossible to stop. The Church now faced questions around who managed the relationship people had with God, who could be close to Him, know Him and reveal the truths of the universe

CHAPTER SIX

THE CITY OF WOE
to
THE HOUSE OF JOY

WHEN and WHERE

AD 1000 -1500

ITALY

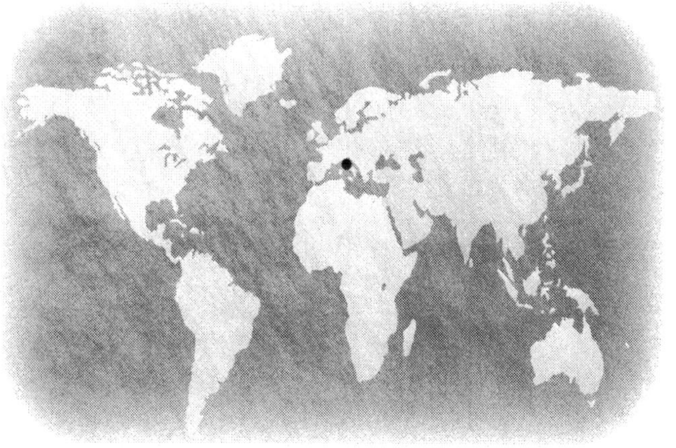

Getting your bearings

Rome was sacked by the Normans in AD 1084, despite this outsider army initially coming to aid the Pope being besieged by the Holy Roman Emperor, King of the Germans. Between the 12th and 15th centuries, Italy played a minor role in the external conflicts taking place. Political life in northern Italy was influenced by two groupings: The Guelph and Ghibelline parties. The former were mainly pro-Pope merchants and the latter were supporters of the Holy Roman Emperor, mainly noblemen. Imperial overlordship ended in AD 1176 when the merchant Lombard League defeated the Germanic Emperor, Frederick Barbarossa.

Italy had significant external relationships, such as those forged with France when Papal rule moved to Avignon in the 1300s. Furthermore, they had significant relationships with the major trading and independent cities in the Flemish areas. The two-way trading relationship and the movement of merchants, artists and craftsmen provided an avenue for the transmission of ideas into Northern Europe.[ccx]

During the first half of the 1500s, the Italian Wars involving all the major states of Western Europe, (France, Spain, the Holy Roman Empire, England, Scotland, the Republic of Venice, the Papal States, and most of the city-states of Italy) as well as the Ottoman Empire, rapidly became a general struggle for power and territory.

Introduction

This chapter describes how alchemy moved out of the shadows during the period of Italian Humanism. Italian city states were very open, and they looked for ideas, particularly from antiquity, to help take their society forward. They looked to a diverse range of sources including ancient Roman civic republicanism, Plato - and alchemy. Through their wealth, city states funded the search for books from many places. Significantly, with the fall of Constantinople to the Ottomans, a new source of ancient texts, including alchemical ones, became available to the West.

"I am the way into the city of woe,
I am the way into eternal pain,
I am the way to go among the lost.

Justice caused my high architect to move,
Divine omnipotence created me,
The highest wisdom, and the primal love.

Before me there were no created things
But those that last forever - as do I.
Abandon all hope you who enter here."

Divine Comedy: Inferno (Hell). Canto III (AD 1320).
Dante Alighieri

The Rise of the City States

Humanism grew out of the Italian independent city states such as Florence, Venice, Milan, Genoa and Sienna. The walled communes from which they emerged were typical of many such enclaves across Europe in the late medieval period and they provided the conditions from which the Humanist movement grew. The Florentine statesman, poet and theorist, Dante Alighieri (AD 1265 – 1321), was a product of this commune system. Another significant factor that gave strength to these states was that Italy only had a marginal role in the conflicts preoccupying key European states at the time – that between Spain and France; the disintegration of the Holy Roman Empire; and the French Hundred Years War with the Kingdom of England (1337 to 1453). The result was that "*...Italy was more or less left in peace during the 15th century.*"[ccxi]

The new city states offered protection and civic organisation for their populations, but the world of Dante was changing. On the one hand, new divisions between merchants and noblemen and between pro and anti-papal alliances were developing. On the positive side, woollen production, trade and banking thrived and levels of literacy and mathematics were high.

Dante exemplified the heights of learning being aspired to in his reading of Latin writers from antiquity and his participation in theological disputes of his day. Alongside these levels of education, a strong spirit of independence prevailed, giving the Italian population a distinct perspective on the world. The ancient Roman Republic, rather than Empires and Emperors, became the model for the aspirations of these growing, prosperous and industrious city states.

Alongside these developments came wealth, patronage, a new movement called Humanism - and a demand for books.

Interpretation of Ancient Texts

As mentioned above, classical texts had already become available in the 1200s, influencing writers and thinkers, such as Dante. Whilst these imports had shaped poetic works like the *Divine Comedy*, a scholastic sensibility and religious virtue was dominant.

Scholars in Padua were the ones to initially break with the old mould of thinking. Scholars, poets, political leaders, lawyers, chancellors, historians and statesmen became involved in reading and interpreting texts. These new Humanists looked to the past to understand ways they might conduct themselves in the present.

Humanism

Marsilius of Padua (AD 1275 – 1342) was committed to political independence and concerned with "*...the harsh yoke of tyrants instead of liberty*"[ccxii] encroaching on society. This was, in part, a patriotic turn in favour of the city states[ccxiii]. Bartolus de Sassoferrato (AD 1313 – 1357) was critical of Aquinas's assumptions that monarchy is always the best form of government. These scholars and jurists focused discussion on early modern constitutionalism, where a monarchy should be decided by election not succession; rule should be by law, not discretion and should be responsive to citizens.

A number of people, including Petrarch (AD 1304 – 1374), generally regarded as the father of humanism, looked to the past to learn how classical republicanism worked. They thought deeply about what the most significant features of the Roman Republic were; not the mechanism of technical government, but the role of the citizenry and what the most suitable conduct was to deliver a just and free society.

They rejected scholasticism which focused on minutiae and trivial dialectical debates.

Humanism would, instead, combine philosophy with a pursuit of eloquence. This should be with an active purpose; for the persuasion of others towards a good political life and peace. Petrarch wanted a return to the 'light' provided by republicanism. Humanists believed that they could be instrumental in bringing this about and this was reflected in the imaginative and resourceful way they set about achieving this. They influenced major figures, such as chancellors and religious figures, including a succession of Popes who, in turn, then brought the Renaissance to Rome.

The writings of the ancient Roman statesman, Cicero, was one influence on these new thinkers. It was Cicero's placing of Virtue and of the status given to the exertion of Man's will over destiny, that the Humanist admired. High regard was given to people using their talent and perusing virtuous action. This effort was to be rewarded with public honour, offered through generous civic celebrations.

Humanists were generally wealthy and self-educated. They used the professional and social positions they held, and the facilities at their disposal, to acquire and copy books and manuscripts they thought would provide guides for their current society. They exemplified their own beliefs by the civic actions they took to influence others. The Church of San Spirito, in Florence, became a centre for discussion in the 1360s and 1370s. They persuaded Cosimo de Medici, from a leading Florentine family at the time, to their cause, and he was instrumental in giving this 'movement of ideas' momentum. He bank-rolled the, often dangerous, task of gathering texts and forgotten manuscripts from all the major towns and monastic libraries across Europe, as well as from Syria and Egypt.[ccxiv]

The culture into which the books arrived in Italy was quite open and fertile, allowing for knowledge and ideas to be developed in new ways. The collections that were brought to Italy laid the foundations for the Renaissance and

> *"...the coming age would see a flowering of both the rational and the irrational, of both sense and nonsense."*[ccxv]

These texts were then housed in, for example, the first public library in Florence based in San Marcos, site of a Dominican monastery.[ccxvi]

> *"Perhaps the best early expression of the modern concept of the public library is to be found in the*

> *establishment of the San Marco library, the first public library at Florence – intended by Niccolò de' Niccoli to be brought 'to the common good, to the public service, to a place open to all, so that all eager for education might be able to harvest from it, as from a fertile field, the rich fruit of learning."*

Opening in 1444, the library contained four hundred volumes, and based on principles of a Renaissance library i.e. its collection was made available to a circle of humanist investigators and the library would be supported by the public patronage. [ccxvii] At its height, the library was said to have included more than 10,000 manuscripts of Ancient Greek, Latin and Hebrew texts[ccxviii].

Whilst in scale, this collection, although impressive, is dwarfed by the scope and scale of what had been housed in the Arabic House of Wisdom or in the library at Córdoba; the latter having in excess of half a million books. However, given the relatively free culture of Italian Republican life it may be that this smaller collection of books had a disproportionate impact on thinking and on the generation of ideas.

The rational and secular turn of thinking is exemplified in **The House of Joy** (La Casa Gioiosa), established in Mantua by Vittorino da Feltre (1378 – 1446)[ccxix]. Here, da Feltre taught what became a hall-mark of humanism, a curriculum of the humanistic subjects - music, art, religion, history, poetry, Greek and Latin, mathematics, religion and philosophy - placing a special emphasis on religious and physical education, with logic assumed rather than being some sort of goal or end-point.

This comprehensive approach to learning and knowledge is also expressed in the idea of the complete man, or *l'uomo universale*, health of body, strength of character, wealth of mind, which was first formulated[ccxx] by Leon Battista Alberti (1404–72)[ccxxi] who said that,

> "...a man can do all things if he will."[ccxxii]

As noted previously, this was a tumultuous period for most of Europe. The fall of Constantinople to the Turks in 1453 is an event of particular importance for this Chapter. And in 1492, Jews were expelled from Spain and the Spanish Inquisition began. Also significant was the invention of the Guttenberg movable type printing press, somewhere between the years 1440 to 1450. This made possible, for the first time, the widespread production and availability of copies of original manuscripts to large numbers of people.

The Return of Plato

Discussions between the Eastern and Western churches also began in this period, partly galvanised by the threat to the Byzantines from the Ottomans. The fall of Constantinople in 1453 was to have an important influence on Italian humanism, as it was followed by a new wave of migration of Byzantine Greek scholars and émigrés into Europe.

One key influence, and of great importance in the distinct development of humanism, was the prominence given to Plato by these migrant scholars. Georgius Gemistus (AD 1355 - 1450/52, aka Plethon) was a Greek Neoplatonist who influenced Cosimo de Medici, inspiring him to fund the establishment of a Platonic Academy in Florence in 1439.

Prior to the translation of Plato's original works, it had been the scholarship of Aristotle and Neoplatonism that had been influential in Western scholasticism. The Italian Humanists, Alberto Rossi and Leonardo Bruni, translated 300 of Greek texts of Aristotle, improving the existing Latin versions available.[ccxxiii] But Petrarch found that whilst his reading of Aristotle left him with more knowledge, it did not change him as a person.

For humanists, the appeal of Plato lay in advocating eloquence, demonstrated using the Socratic argument. The consequence was virtuous, a persuasion of others towards moral goodness.

This approach combined the civic and Christian beliefs of humanists. From a theological perspective, moral knowledge could be fully known through the exercise of civil and canon law. However, there was still the belief that the attainment of certain knowledge of nature and its causes, was ultimately beyond human capabilities[ccxxiv].

However, others, such as Theodore Gaza (AD 1398 - 1475) from Macedonia, continued to promote the centrality of Aristotle and, from 1447, Gaza taught at the newly established university in Ferrara.

Matters of Reason; Matters of Irrationality

The following section explores examples of how the humanists began to interpret and use the new material available to them.

In addition to the Humanist focus on the Humanities, the industriousness of the city states resulted in new thinking around optics, astronomy, astrology, mathematics and perspective. These disciplines became more integrated into civic projects which also resulted in greater involvement of specialist artisans, architects and artists.

One example that convinced Humanists of the practical, rather than metaphysical, value of mathematical and natural knowledge, arose through a multi-disciplinary collaboration between the architect Filippo Brunelleschi (1377) and the young mathematics student, Paulo Toscanelli (AD 1397 – 1482). Toscanelli worked with Brunelleschi on the popular topic of perspective and, through this, Brunelleschi made a major discovery related to optics, architecture and perspective - linear perspective. He then taught this to the artist Masaccio. Combining different disciplines through active work brought a transformation in painting, sculpture, the training of artists and a new literature on painting. [ccxxv]

The relationship between moral and natural philosophy was also tested in this changing society. There was a shift towards greater consideration of the natural, spiritual world which was, in part, a consequence of the availability of the writings associated with the ancient Egyptian/Greek god, Hermes Trismegistus. Cosimo de Medici had instructed Leonardo de Candia to bring the ancient *Corpus Hermetica* (the 42 books of knowledge) to Italy when Constantinople fell to the Turks.[ccxxvi] Hermes Trismegistus, as mentioned in Chapters 2 and 3, was believed to have been an Egyptian/Greek god. The reputation of Hermes was already established through the writings of the early Church fathers and associations with Islamic astrology and through an Arab variation of the text that had been translated into Latin by Hugo von Santalla, from Northern Spain[ccxxvii]

Marsillo Ficino (AD 1433 – 1499), Neoplatonist and astrologer, saw within the texts, some parallels with Christian scripture and Platonic cosmology.[ccxxviii] Under instruction from Cosimo, Ficino translated fourteen of the books from Greek to Latin and, when published in 1463, it went under the title the *Pymander*.

Significantly, Ficino, who was the first to translate the original works of Plato from Greek to Latin, was also head of the Platonic Academy in Florence. He aimed to integrate some of these ancient ideas into Christian theology.

Through a synthesis of Hermeticism and Platonism, Ficino developed a belief that there was a trapped spirit within Man which had divine intellect. Through spiritual contemplation, Man was able to emulate God's creativity, sharing in the governing of the world and determining the course of future events.[ccxxix]

The influx of ideas, funded by a powerful patron, provided the Humanists with approval to study a wide range of topics including the occult sciences, alchemy, magic and astrology. Kabbalah, originating from within Judaism and seeking to uncover new depths of meaning in scripture, was another source investigated. It became established as a practice in Southern France and Northern Spain around the 12th and 13th centuries. This practice was then embraced by Francesco Giorgi (1466 – 1540) as a part of Christianity.

Knowledge of both nature and of the supernatural were viewed as two parts of a whole and there was a strong and favourable receptiveness to these many writings. Not only did these texts provide new authority to some ancient natural philosophy, they also implied a different, and more important, place for Man in the world.

Like Ficino, Pico della Mirandola (AD 1433 – 1499) combined the rational with the mystical and he was strongly influenced by alchemy. At the age of just twenty-three, he produced his nine hundred theses, known as '*The Oration on the Dignity of Man*'. This work mixed philosophy and religion, becoming known as the Manifesto of the Renaissance. One of his aims was to try to help to reconcile the schools of Aristotle and Plato. Mirandola also advocated the learning of Hebrew and gaining knowledge of Talmudic sources because of their common relationship with Christianity and the Old Testament.

Putting on Wings – Dedalus and Icarus

What becomes clear from the brief investigation for this chapter, is that Humanists had a strong belief that Man could participate in his own transformation; altering what it means to be human. The flood of ideas, which called on both human reason and the human spirit, resulted in a change within Man's imagination. Goodrick-Clarke (2008) suggests that Mirandola saw Man's true greatness lying in his freedom to become whatever he wished to be. Where God made animals and angels with fixed natures and a fixed place in the universe, He gave Man alone no fixed abode, form, or function - and free from such limitations, Man has the power to change, develop, make and mould himself.[ccxxx]

Man's ability to perfect nature was one expression of this. Some, like the alchemist Peter Bonus (c.AD 1300), who produced the alchemical text *Precious New Pearl* (*Margarita Preciosa Novella*), continued in the same vein as Paul of Taranto, (late 1200s), placing the perfective art of alchemy alongside the professional art of medicine due to its capacity to bring about change in matter. [ccxxxi]

There were several people during this period who tested mystical ideas through experimentation, some with alchemy and others focused on the darker, occult arts. In France, Nicolas Flamel (c. AD 1340 – 1418), a scribe and manuscript seller, devoted his life to finding the Philosopher's Stone, a substance believed to be capable of transmuting baser metals into gold or silver and which was also believed to be able to prolong life. There was Bernard Trevisan (AD 1406 – 1490), an Italian alchemist who travelled extensively, partly driven by his search for the Philosopher's Stone. And there was the grisly Breton Occultist Knight Gilles de Rais (c. AD 1405 – 1440), a companion of Joan of Arc, working in the darker areas of the spiritual world. He complied with the instructions of an Italian alchemist he had employed, who told him that to placate a demon summoned by an alchemist, the body parts of a dead child should be offered. This occult practice was to become a habit of de Rais, for which he was eventually caught, tried and hanged.

Decline of Humanist Republicanism

The centrality of public citizenship during the Florentine Republic lessened. Philosophers, such as Mirandola and Ficino, gradually withdrew, spending more time in private contemplation. Although scholars had initially found wealthy patrons in the Medici, and the new curriculum was adopted widely, Humanism was unable to build a stronger movement to sustain Republicanism and civic involvement.

The concept of Virtue also changed bringing a shift in its meaning. Initially, the emphasis, revived by the early Humanists, had been on man's courage pitted against the capricious god, Fortuna. But later, the concept of Virtue became weighted down with pessimism. The contest between Virtue and Fortuna became a metaphor for a kind of dual taking place between a lone individual who is pitted against his wider community that is not acting virtuously. [ccxxxii]

These shifts coincided with the Country starting to face new threats. Ludovico Sforza, Duke of Milan, seeking allies, suggested to Charles VIII of France that he should press his claim to the throne of Naples. Charles obliged and launched an invasion of the peninsula in 1494. Although, in this instance, he was forced to leave, invasions by his successors continued until 1559. Reacting to these early invasions some, like the Dominican Savonarola (AD 1452 – 1498), launched a strident defence of the Republic, presenting it as a struggle for religious freedom.[ccxxxiii]

Although humanism remained marginal, the underlying drive to elevate Man, reason and the individual's relationship to wider society, did ensure some distinct elements of an organised civic life, with virtue at its core, continued. Over the years, knowledge became more widely dispersed within Italian culture. By the 1540s, women, for example, began to emerge as respected writers and published works for the first time. Their involvement in literature began with the founding of literary salons in Naples, Venice, Rome, Siena, and Florence where they organised notable poets and writers, both male and female, to come together to read and discuss their work.[ccxxxiv]

The sad, and somewhat, pathetic case of Giovanni (Mercurio) da Corregio (c. AD 1450s), can be taken to symbolise the demise of Humanism. He was probably a mythical character and said to be from a noble background. He abandoned his position for the lure of the mythical world of hermeticism and alchemy. He became an eloquent, apocalyptic preacher and writer, wandering between Italian cities, believing himself to be the Son of God with hermetic wisdom. He aimed to persuade others of his gifts, including the Pope, possibly with the aim of securing some income, but he ended up destitute.

The relatively brief moment of Italian humanism was an important catalyst for the Renaissance. It created an important spark and reconsideration of how Man saw himself. Through the authority of ancient alchemical texts, the idea was adopted that Man had a divine intellect and, this spark within him would allow him to know the Divine God.

Was Man dabbling in a form of hubris, as portrayed in the Greek mythological story of Dedalus and Icarus who presumed, like the gods, they could fly? Or was this new confidence warranted? Maybe it was Man, not alchemy, that was finally moving out of the shadows. Ficino's belief that Man could comprehend divine nature, propelled both Man and alchemy forward, to be taken up by Northern European Humanists.

CHAPTER SEVEN

THE CABINET OF CURIOSITIES (THE KUNSTKAMMER)

WHEN and WHERE

AD 1400 –1612

BUDAPEST • BASEL • WITTENBERG • LONDON • PRAGUE

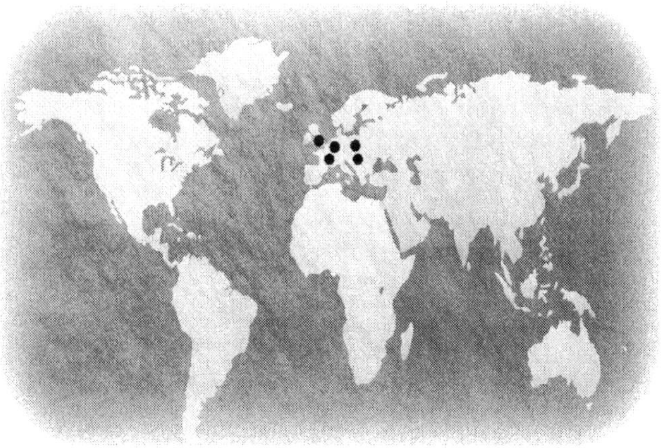

Getting your bearings

This was a time of economic transformation and changes in systems of organising agriculture, the economy and finance. It was a period where the Kingdoms of Northern Europe, historically self-sufficient, began to look outwards, finding ways to access the products and trade from China, India and Asia. In addition to trading across continents, this was a period of major exploration, with the voyages of discovery around Africa and to America taking place, allowing the development of new foreign relationships, trade and the creation of several colonies.

In addition to the multiple crusades that had taken place to try to retain control over the near East, Christian rule faced other external challenges as secular power increased within the kingdoms. The Church also faced internal challenges to its authority and teachings. This resulted in major dislocations in diplomatic relationships and the Reformation; a major split within official religion. The Church reacted using repression, special papal courts (known as the Inquisition) and by a radical re-thinking of theology.

Introduction

This chapter explores the entry of Humanism into Northern Europe, unleashing controversies that began to reshape society in new, dramatic ways. Alchemy and magic were significant within the public imagination and were having an impact across society.

The chapter describes the unravelling of the threads that had held together a view of the universe and the heavens. It is also about the essential nature of Man. The light and optimistic Italian Humanist interpretation of classical texts found its way northwards via various trading routes and through religious and political relationships. The mood in Northern Europe was, in contrast, dark, preoccupied with Man's fall in the Garden of Eden and how it might be possible to return to a prelapsarian state. Alchemy, taken seriously by both the Church and the royal courts, was seen to potentially hold the key to reversing this.

However, before looking at radical changes in religious belief, this chapter looks briefly at the way knowledge was incorporated throughout society in new libraries and it explores how traditional hierarchy was challenged through new conceptions of knowledge, education and cosmologies. This is a period of great contrasts and high stakes, where one's beliefs around the mysteries of life and the spiritual world acquired an intense level of importance.

New Houses of Libraries and the Dispersal of Knowledge

The last two chapters have established that, generally, it was a demand for new thinking that created a demand for books. These texts provided the raw material from which the Renaissance and the Reformation emerged.

So where were all these books housed and who had access to them?

Ancient and Arabic texts imported into Europe through Church sponsorship had already filled Cathedral and monastic libraries. New types of libraries, distinct from the older church ones, also sprang up. Initially, these were created in Italian city states, such as in Verona, Naples, the Vatican and Florence and then in Northern Europe, in places such as Fontainebleau, France and the Bibliotheca Corviniana in Budapest, Hungary. The latter was one of the most renowned libraries of the Renaissance.

The library in Fontainebleau followed the Italian model of both design and layout but added a new feature: a law was passed requiring printers to deposit a free copy of every new book produced into the regal library.[ccxxxv]

These new libraries began holding collections from antiquity, meaning that monasteries were no longer the only places such texts could be found thus breaking the theological monopoly the Church had over knowledge.

Some libraries, even if still located in churches, incorporated a new educational element, becoming part of town life. The earliest example of such a library is believed to have been established in 1413 in Brunswick, now part of Northern Germany.[ccxxxvi]

An additional and important factor assisting the general dispersal of knowledge into mainstream society was the invention of the Guttenberg movable type printing press, sometime between 1440 to 1450. This dispersal was further aided by institutions like the Sorbonne in Paris introducing a printing press. There was also an increase in translation of texts into the vernacular.

Northern European Humanists - Free Will, Education and the Limits of Knowledge

The hierarchical structures governing Northern Europe at the time shaped how new ideas were received and interpreted. Compared to Italian Humanism, the experience within Northern Europe was very different. Ancient cosmological thinking had been incorporated within the Church to justify the positions of those holding a higher status.[ccxxxvii] In Germany, France and England, the grip of the Church, with its nine levels of ecclesiastical hierarchy, had a deep and profound influence on how people saw themselves.

Nevertheless, despite the rigid structure of many Northern European societies, the north-ward travel and dissemination of humanist ideas contributed to a breakout of theological controversies akin to those that had occurred at different time within Christianity. The Church retained some of the best intellectual minds of the time and discussions around the relationship of the individual to God, how divinity operates through the material world, and the processes by which Man might understand this were played out again.

A couple of key individuals from the time illustrate how knowledge was being used to challenge Church orthodoxies.

Thomas More (AD 1478–1535), an English lawyer and statesman, and the Dutch scholar Desiderius Erasmus (AD 1466 – 1536), were friends. Erasmus introduced More to the literary networks of Northern humanism.[ccxxxviii] Both were engaged in a revival of the Greek language and examined the social possibilities of education, believing that it benefitted the individual and that it engendered good government.

In his book, *Utopia*, of 1516, More imagines a society where the current European Christian institutions, driven by self-interest, are replaced by ones governed by reason. Erasmus determined that education was of central importance for the development of human self-improvement and for the exercise of reasoned free-will.

Erasmus possessed, and studied in detail, original Greek scripture and he was involved in the development of new disciplines such as philology - the study of the historical development of language and literature. Through his research he revealed inconsistency and error within scripture, opening the possibility of new interpretations of holy texts.

At Cambridge, which was to become a key institution behind Protestantism in the 16th century, Erasmus produced a new translation of the Bible from original manuscript; a task that had not been undertaken in over one thousand years. Up until this point, the official Christian text was *The Vulgate of St Jerome*, held by the Church to be the sole custodian of God's word. In his New Testament, first published in 1515, Erasmus placed Greek and Latin texts side by side so they could be directly compared. Mistakes in previous Latin translations were revealed for all to see. The inquiring mind of Erasmus had started to break the Vatican's monopoly and this New Testament was to be used by Luther and Tyndall for their own Bible translations.

However, this break in authority was still within the context of loyalty to the Church. Both More and Erasmus believed that successful individual conduct could only be achieved by reference to orthodoxy and within some form of official constraint. Erasmus advocated *Docta pietas* (learned piety) as a means of determining where the limit of human understanding should be. He warned against *Impia curiositas* (unholy inquisitiveness). He privileged ethics over logic and the formation of character over factual knowledge."[ccxxxix]

> *"Embrace what you are allowed to perceive; venerate from afar what you are not allowed to*

> *perceive and look in awe and with simple faith on whatever it is that is concealed from you. Keep far away from impia curiositas .”*

More, like Erasmus, also believed in the need for constraint. Rummel (2017) explains,

> *“Against Tyndale's “feeling faith”, inspired by the Spirit in the heart of the individual, More argued that the Spirit operates through the medium of the church (CWM 8:2, 752–53).”*[ccxl]

Others, like Martin Luther (AD 1483 – 1536), were spurred on in their belief, not by civic humanism, but by looking back to the writings of early Christian thinkers, the Church Fathers and scripture. Augustine’s theology had become popular over the preceding two centuries and became a voice of authority for the Reformation.[ccxli]

Luther began studying Augustine from around 1509. Luther believed a relationship with God should be a more direct one, attained through reading the scripture. This would bypass church hierarchy. Luther shared More’s belief that the Grace of God, rather than free will, played a greater part in the determination of a Man’s destiny.

The general public were also being given more consideration than they had previously, but this was not framed as civic humanism, as in Italy, but instead discussed as Christian piety.

By the 1520s, a new movement, Protestantism, grew out of some of these controversies. Protestantism was initially defined through the protest made by some princes and representatives from fourteen of the German Imperial free city states against restrictions on Lutheran teachings and worship. This theological protest was made at the Diet of Worms to the Holy Roman Emperor to whom the city states answered. It then became a political and social movement, growing in Northern Europe against the hierarchical grip of the Church and the powers of the Holy Roman Emperor.

Old and New Cosmologies – Macrocosm and Microcosm

Discussions concerning the heaven and earth retained elements of past systems, but gradually started to pose new questions.

In terms of continuity, during the Medieval scholastic period, there had been a re-emergence of early Christian thinking and discussions about the physical universe and scientific systems. The works of Aristotle provided the scientific material shaping late medieval thinking. As discussed in Chapter 5, Albert the Great (c. AD 1200 - 1280) and Thomas Aquinas (AD 1225 - 1274) were two figures influential in the incorporation of Aristotle into Christian orthodoxy. Aristotle and the liberal arts also became core to teaching within the medieval universities.

However, whilst central to Western theology and university life, the validity of Aristotle's system of ideas began to be tested.

Mathematics and astronomy began to present challenges to key theological and hierarchical assumptions. Whether they had intended to or not, the endeavours of people like Nicolaus Copernicus (AD 1473 – 1543), Tycho Brahe (AD 1546 – 1601), Giordano Bruno (AD 1548 – 1600) and Rene Descartes (AD 1596 – 1650) raised questions about the universe, cosmos and heavenly bodies.

Nicolaus Copernicus (AD 1473 – 1543), from the Prussian Kingdom of Poland, was a mathematician and astronomer. He had been, by all accounts, schooled by a professor of Aristotelian philosophy and then received further education on canon law and astronomy in Italy. Copernicus developed a system which placed the Sun, rather than the Earth, at the centre of the universe. Although he was not entirely original in this formulation, as Aristarchus of Samos had formulated such a model some eighteen centuries earlier, it is likely that he came to this conclusion independently.[ccxlii]

When considering his breakthrough work at a conceptual level, alongside that of the ancient Ptolemaic system in use, his system could have been viewed as just an alternative, but equivalent, calculating system for predicting the positions of the planets, the moon and the sun. But Copernicus's key audience, the class of medical-astrologers, did not view it like this, finding his system incompatible with their fundamental, rational, beliefs based on

> *"...a hierarchical spatial ordering of the cosmos from the highest Divine sphere to the lowest terrestrial sphere."*[ccxliii]

One hundred years later, Tycho Brahe (AD 1546 – 1601), felt the disquieting impact of a world thrown out of harmony by new discoveries – a disquiet, in this instance, caused by his own investigations.

> *"On November 11, 1572, he suddenly saw a "new star," brighter than Venus and where no star was supposed to be, in the constellation Cassiopeia."*[ccxliv]

This discovery was very unsettling because the intellectual community, up until this point, believed in the rational Aristotelian doctrine of inner and continuous harmony of the unchanging world, ruled by the stars, which created a system of belief based on order. This order of ideas also created a method of self-preservation for this intellectual community. However, the appearance of this new star, in a place it was not meant to be, undermined the laws of antiquity by proving they were not immutable.

In the face of the challenge of the new Copernican system, Brahe utilised some of Copernicus's technical improvements whilst retaining the Earth at the centre of the universe; adjusting, but fundamentally preserving, the status quo.[ccxlv]

The Italian Giordano Bruno (AD 1548 – 1600) was, in contrast to Brahe, not content to stay tied to some middle ground. Born within a few years of Brahe, and schooled in Humanism and Aristotle, Bruno cast his net wide, taking in the panoply of ideas circulating in the late Renaissance period. He was a controversialist, travelling and teaching in Northern Europe, moving from court to court, gaining funding as he went.

People like Bruno began to develop new systems that corresponded with how they believed the universe to be. Brahe's new star, and other discoveries, were sending ancient Aristotelian thinking off-kilter. Old systems no longer represented the new world people were observing.

Within Aristotle's system there were distinct super and sub-lunary parts to the universe - with the super-lunary element (the celestial bodies in the heavens) being infinite, unchanging and moving in fixed, circular motion compared to the universe, including the earth, which was finite, moving in a fixed linear motion and changing through generation and corruption.[ccxlvi]

For Bruno, the appearance of a new star demonstrated that the heavens *do* generate matter and also showed that fire, one of the four elements of the sub-lunary universe, also *existed in the heavens.*

These conclusions obliterated the sharp line that had existed between the heavens and the universe that had endured for centuries. One further shift was that Bruno also created a radically different view of what constituted space. Knox (2019) explains that Bruno, channelling the Italian humanists take on Hermes Trismegistus, believed,

> " *atoms were incorporeal spheres with spatial locations. Soul, working through the intermediary of aether or spirit, joined these incorporeal, identical, spheres to make a body. Indeed, they were not so much components as instances of the universe.*"

In Bruno's conception there could be no natural hierarchy or centre and, importantly, the incorporeal, active elements of spirit and soul were key new elements within Bruno's system.[ccxlvii]

Unfortunately for Bruno, whether directly or indirectly due to his heretical beliefs, he fell out with an Italian patron. He found himself the victim of the Roman inquisition, being burnt at the stake in Rome, with his tongue and mouth gruesomely, and symbolically, fixed to prevent any further heretical words being uttered.

A further, and important example of the radical shifts in thinking, is that of Descartes (AD 1596 – 1650). He drew on the ideas of the Greek atomists (Chapter 1). He believed that during the Creation, a coalescence of particles resulted in the formation of just one type of matter, making up both the heavens and the earth; again removing the Aristotelian distinction between these two realms. On matter, drawing on some of the ideas of Leucippus and Democritus, Descartes thought matter had no active forms – unlike Bruno. He concluded that matter operated through three laws of motion, with God determining the way matter reacted to other matter.

The dissolving of the distinction between physics and metaphysics had a profound influence, opening a pathway for new theories.[ccxlviii]

The thorny questions these new observations and theories raised, fundamentally challenged Christian Orthodoxy and broke the long-standing classical systems that had shaped belief for centuries. Key questions posed were:

On God and Man - Where was God's physical place in the cosmos? And If the earth was not at the centre of God's creation, where did that leave Man? And after centuries of belief in a clear separation between the heavens and earth, in what now made the heavens different and unique?[ccxlix]

And on the cosmos - If perfection, which was represented in the mathematical seven, now had to be eleven, following Galileo's discovery of the four moons of Jupiter, where did that leave the ancient mystical understandings of the cosmos?

Despite the consequences for the individuals who held such challenging views, their thinking and ideas about physics and cosmology began to have an impact on Church thinking and its hierarchy.

Purifying the Soul – Magic and Alchemy

These unsettling observations and shifts in thinking took place alongside some fundamental discussions about the scope of Man's freedom to act, the nature of free will and of Man's nature following his Fall in the Garden of Eden.

Aspects of magic were also more widely discussed, and interpretations of whether it was a force for good or for evil developed. Strong symbolism, using light and darkness, came in to play.

The use and application of knowledge and magic were often closely related, but also revealed great differences in underlying belief and philosophy between Italian and Northern European thinking. Germany was at the heart of many of the Northern European discussions.

> *"As the Protestant mind focused on the frailty of man and sought the western esoteric traditions of salvation through piety and close attention to God's Word in the Bible, the self-confident magic of the Florentine Neoplatonists seemed sheer hubris. Once at home in the sunlit world of Renaissance Italy, the magus and voyager through higher worlds assumed a darker aspect in the northern, Germanic world."*[ccl]

Renaissance Hermeticism, Kabbala and the ideas of Marsilio Ficino (AD 1433 – 1499) and Pico della Mirandola (AD 1469 – 1493) were brought into Germany by the famous Hebrew scholar Johann Reuchlin (AD 1455–1522)[ccli],[cclii] and Henry Cornelius Agrippa (AD 1486 – 1535) – both Germans.

Agrippa was the most influential writer of Renaissance esoterica and Western occultism of the time. Agrippa believed that Man, due to original sin, had lost his power over nature. A magus (priest), however, could achieve a purified soul, attain a true understanding of God's revelation, gain mastery over his own body and win power over all of nature.[ccliii] Agrippa wrote three books, but his ideas were denounced as heretical by the Dominican Inquisitor, Conrad Köllin of Ulm.

Into this mix was a transformation in how witches, magic and mystical practices were seen.

Firstly, the conception of witches changed. Folk magic had been part of pagan practice in many local communities in Europe, where it was believed certain people were able to, for example, cure disease or counter malevolent sorcery. However, resulting from some of the seeds Thomas Aquinas had sewn on *maleficium,* communities were become less tolerant of witches.

High magic on the other hand, was becoming more popular amongst learned men. This high magic emerged during the Renaissance, drawing on ancient philosophies and stories influenced by Neoplatonism and Hermeticism. Elite circles rehabilitated and adapted this pre-Christian, eastern magus[ccliv]. It was theoretically complex, and it saw the practice of magic as part of a wider spiritual system. One aim of the intellectual discussions was the creation of a new defence of hierarchy that could be achieved through the incorporation of magic and alchemy within esoteric ideas. This elite protection of knowledge contrasted with wider cultural developments aiding the growth of printing houses and the proliferation of ideas through the provision of direct public access to cheap print copies of non-Latin sacred scripture and a host of other texts and pamphlets.

The Soul and Darkness

The dark aspects of alchemy and magic, linked to people's inner natures, were very influential within the imaginations of Protestant scholars and theologians, particularly in Germany.

Luther, and the Church more generally, did not share the positive, humanist view about the Will of Man. Instead, they reasserted orthodoxy, informed by their deep-seated mystical views about what caused nature to deliver such things as plague and crop failure.

Here a quote from Luther's Tabletalk, showing alchemy as metaphor, provides an example.

> *"For, as in a furnace the fire extracts and separates from a substance the other portions,*

> *and carries upward the spirit, the life, the sap, the strength, while the unclean matter, the dregs, remain at the bottom, like a dead and worthless carcass." (Luther: Tabletalk)*[cclv]

Old stories and folklore took on new, darker meanings with alchemy and magic now appearing. By the late sixteenth century, Ficino's priest-physician and Pico's "miracle of man" had given way to the figure of Faust, a necromancer who sold his soul to the devil.

The character of Agrippa, mentioned earlier in this chapter, was shaped by malicious legends perpetrated by hostile and credulous monks. His memory soon became entwined with the story of Faust.[cclvi]

Printing meant new versions of old stories spread quickly. The Faust story circulated in Germany in the late 1400s and remained popular for decades. One version of this tale was published by the Frankfurt publishing house of Johann Spies. Significantly, the Spies Imprint was printed in 1587, during the period when the major Witch Trials of Trier, Germany, took place (between 1581 to 1593). These trials were probably the biggest in European history at this time and resulted in the death of at least 368 people.[cclvii]

Faust symbolised the fate of Man, driven by a passion for knowledge, like the biblical Adam and Eve - or a man like Bruno. By not respecting the boundaries of knowledge, defined by those like Erasmus, Man's quest for knowledge consigns him to perpetual perdition.

In the 'Spies' book,

> *"...Dr Faustus was fain to love forbidden things, after which he hankered night and day, taking unto himself the wings of an eagle in order to search out the uttermost parts of heaven and earth;... yea like unto that evil angel who opposed God, as was cast off by God on account of his arrogance and presumption."*[cclviii]

This was a sentiment that inspired or was, at least, shared by Kings. The Stewart king, James VI of Scotland, later also becoming James I of England (James VI/I) exemplified such a monarch. James's book *Daemonologie*, was written in 1597, ten years after the Spies imprint was published. James writes,

> *"...and so mounting from degree to degree, vpon the slipperie and vncertain scale of curiositie; they are at last entised, that where lawfull artes or sceinces failes, to satisfie their restles mindes, even to seeke to that black and vnlawfull science of Magie.*[cclix]

Between 1550 – 1650 there was a notable surge in alchemical and medico-chemical publishing within Europe. [cclx] The search for how to redeem corrupted matter and return the entire world back to its pristine, prelapsarian state was a hope driving this trend in alchemical practice.[cclxi]

Heinrich Khunrath (AD 1560 – 1605), for example, practised philosophical alchemy, a spiritual art undertaken by pious people concerned with finding out God's secrets and seeking cures for the ills created due to the fall of man.

The Soul and the Light

The gloom and darkness within the underlying ideas of the Church was, nevertheless, challenged by several people who perceived society differently and, in their hands, alchemy might play a part in how life could be improved.

One cause of the rapid diffusion of alchemy is attributed to the controversial figure of Paracelsus (AD 1493–1541 aka Theophrastus), a pioneer of chemical medicine, whose thought and practice was grounded in the mix of ideas of the day, spanning old and new world concepts. [cclxii]

Whilst darkness greatly influenced the times, the open minds of those like Paracelsus presented new and expansive possibilities within the "*the latent forces of Nature.*" He wrote,

> *He who is born in imagination discovers the latent forces of Nature.... Besides the stars that are established, there is yet another – imagination - that begets a new star and a new heaven.*[cclxiii]

Paracelsus grew up in a mining area located in southern Austria, a place where the education of children was based around mining, metals and smelting. Paracelsus had exposure to a variety of ideas including Arabic practical science, alchemy, philosophy and a fusion of mystical and rational ideas that were informing late Renaissance Christianity. He was schooled specifically in medicine, surgery and physics.

Aged sixteen, he studied medicine at the Universities of Basel and Vienna and gained his doctorate degree from the University of Ferrara[cclxiv], a place where he was free to express his rejection of the prevailing view that the stars and the planets controlled all the parts of the human body.[cclxv]

Back in Basel ten years later, he worked as a physician and taught at the University; a scholarly centre for Renaissance Humanism, where he mixed with people like Erasmus. It is in Basel that he apparently acquired the nickname, "the Luther of Physicians," pinning a program of his bold forthcoming lectures to the notice board of the University. He then invited the public, students and artisan barber surgeons to the lectures, delivering them in German, not Latin. The lectures, attended by large and enthusiastic audiences, were delivered by Paracelsus wearing an alchemist's leather apron rather than a traditional academic gown.

Paracelsus reordered the classical Greek conceptions of Macrocosm and Microcosm around the Hermetic premise of the universes being constituted "*As Above, So Below*", bringing together practices including astrology, alchemy and sacred geometry as well as some of the new conceptions of the universe and the heavens. His alchemy and laboratory processes were directly connected "*...to the material world he grew up in with its mining, smelting and associated processes*"[cclxvi], providing a real-world impetus to the development of laboratory experimentation and exploration of the material world.

Rather than using the traditional theories of Hippocrates and Galen, whom he denounced as antiquated, or the books handed down to him, he lectured on practical and theoretical medicine and things he had discovered and learnt through his own work and experience. He overthrew convention by publicly burning the books of Ibn-Sina and Galen, an act of defiance against authority at a time when the work and teaching of these scholars were held to be unalterable and inviolable, and where the slightest deviation from their teachings was regarded as nothing short of heretical.[cclxvii]

His new controversial methods led to his expulsion from the City. [cclxviii;cclxix] Some of the challenging ideas he developed include:

- evidence gained through one's own senses should be the basis of a pious Christian faith;
- to the four elements of earth, fire, water and air should be added an astrological world of the planets with their corresponding materials for example, Saturn/Mars corresponding with Mercury/Sulphur [cclxx];

- balance in human life achieved through an internal balance of the four humours should be replaced with a new method where external factors, and their effects on an individual, are taken into account;
- the authority of the physician Galen should be challenged as he never attended the bedside of those being treated. He despised those trading herbal remedies based on Galenic theory [cclxxi] replacing these with new chemical remedies he developed and believed to be more promising. [cclxxii]

His focus on the impact the material world had on people, and how matter is connected and inter-related, led to his search for specific cures and remedies for significant diseases and disorders. One example is his cure for the "miners' disease" (silicosis), which he believed resulted from inhaling metal vapours, rather than being a punishment for sin administered by mountain spirits[cclxxiii]. Another was his use of the metal mercury for the treatment of syphilis. And, Paracelsus gives us the idea of "what makes a man ill also cures him", by using tiny samples of a person's excreta within a remedy administered to cure the Plague that was rife in the area he came from.[cclxxiv]

Another person, Alexander Von Suchten, (AD 1520 – 1575) from Gdansk, Poland, also discovered "*many flaws in Galenic medicine*" and he embraced Theophrastus's [i.e. Paracelsus's] teachings. He utilised alchemy, "*...devoting himself to iatrochemical*[2] *laboratory practice.*"[cclxxv]

Bruno, coming later than Luther and Paracelsus, reflected on the range of accumulated new ideas. He overturned other key elements of classical Aristotelian philosophy. Where Aristotle had believed that the first principles, the most dignified "theoretical" sciences, were beyond human capacity to alter, Bruno thought that this passivity towards nature was a problem shared by Christian teachings which had reinterpreted ancient teaching as being derived from divine and immutable laws. Bruno took a contrary view and believed that the gods gave Man both intelligence and hands for a purpose:

> *"This capacity consists not only in the power to work in accordance with nature and the usual course of things, but beyond that and outside her laws, to the end that by fashioning, or having the power to fashion, other natures, other orders by the means of his intelligence, with that freedom without which his resemblance to the deity would not exist, he might in the end make himself god of the earth."*[cclxxvi]

Alchemy – Aiding Transformation

With the backdrop of the previous sections on the light and dark perceptions of Man, this section indicates

---

[2] Originating in alchemy, Iatrochemistry used chemicals to treat disease. https://www.merriam-webster.com/medical/iatrochemistry

how alchemy began to shape day to day activities and practices.

There was a commercial, practical alchemy, relating to medicine and metallurgy. Recipes for use in the transmutation of metals into gold were traded and many people worked in the laboratories that had become established, particularly across the areas of the Holy Roman Empire. [cclxxvii]

The patronage of scholars working in this field started to come from merchants and bankers rather than from princes and kings. Patronage now often focused on practical problems relating to, for example, craft, art, architecture, medicine, navigation and the techniques of alchemy. These new relationships elevated the experimental and practical activity used in the pursuit of knowledge for utility.[cclxxviii]

But the traditional relationship of scholars and others to the established hierarchy did not disappear but, instead, flourished. Englishman John Dee (AD 1527 – 1608/9) is one such scholar who worked within the Royal Court in England. He was friendly with Elizabeth I's upper circle and, significantly, he had the ear of the Queen herself, using astrology to set the date of her coronation (15th January 1559). He proposed a national library and revisions to the English calendar.[cclxxix]

The position and influence of Dee and the status of alchemy, astrology and magic were being utilised within establishment circles and the Royal Court to show off the Kingdom and increase its stature.

Dee was the son of a merchant from London who went to Cambridge and then, later, to Oxford. He had been an industrious student and some of his knowledge of natural philosophy developed from Arabic and medieval science. He travelled extensively, studied, taught (including on Euclid in Paris), and made connections with many people throughout Europe. He amassed thousands of items and books, creating the largest library in England. He was skilled in mathematics and in its applications within cartography, navigation, cryptography, alchemy and astrology. He trained principal navigators that were heading off on England's voyages of discovery to North America and the northern coasts of Europe. Martin Frobisher, Walter Raleigh and his brothers, were trained by Dee.

Yet, despite the range of Dee's knowledge, his main interest was to learn how to commune with angels. It does not come as a surprise to find that Shakespeare may have modelled the character Prospero from the Tempest on John Dee.

But alchemy also attracted many charlatans. With a focus on the transmutation of base metals to gold and magic, alchemy was always open to forgery and trickery carried out by imposters, several of whom were operating within the Courts across Europe.[cclxxx]

Edward Kelley (AD 1555 – 1597) may well have been one of these imposters, but he was also the person Dee believed would be able to contact the angels for him using a scryer, or crystal-gazer. For Dee, contact with the angels wasn't a mere personal quest, but something with far bolder aims. Dee and Kelley held seances that included

> "*prayers for enlightenment ... in the spirit of Dee's ecumenical hopes that alchemy and angelic knowledge would heal the rift of Christendom*".[cclxxxi]

Dee also believed that the angels held knowledge that would aid the English in their discoveries of new and uncharted lands on Earth.[cclxxxii] Kelley also claimed to possess the secret of how to transmute base metals into gold, the goal of alchemy. He managed to find influence and wealth in the court of Rudolph II located in Prague.

Robert Fludd (AD 1574 – 1637), was another possible opportunist, combining characteristics of the polymath Dee, and the chancer Kelley.[cclxxxiii]

Basil Valentine, supposedly from the 1400s (c. AD 1394 – 1450), is named as the author of a widely reproduced alchemical book, *The Twelve Keys of Basil Valentine*, which discusses general alchemical principles and the required process steps. The book was not, however, published until 1599 (it was probably a work by its publisher, Johann Thölde, AD 1565–1624). The book was written in veiled language and used allegorical text and related images.[cclxxxiv] Only a knowledgeable reader, or an expert adept in alchemical practice, was expected to be able to interpret it.

Reaction to Alchemy by the Catholic Church Hierarchy and The Royal Courts

The concluding part of this chapter focuses on how the Catholic Church and the royal courts responded to new questions and a changing culture that started to embrace a much greater mix of ideas.

The Responses of the Catholic Church Hierarchy

How did the Catholic Church respond to challenges against hierarchy?

The Catholic Church hierarchy had concerns about alchemy, but its views were contradictory.

One of the concerns, as already mentioned, was that improved technical know-how meant an age-old concern about the possibilities of fraudulent coinage became even stronger. A Papal decree of 1317 allowed people to be fined for fraudulent alchemical practice and, in 1488, this practice was forbidden due to concerns about counterfeit gold being produced.

However, the Church was not consistent in its approach with exceptions being made and a varied application of the law. For example, Giovanni Agostino Panteo (also, Joannes Pantheus or Pantaura), was a Venetian alchemist and priest. In 1519, with the permission of both the Pope and of the Council of Ten in Venice, he published the book *Ars transmutationis metallicae* (Art of metallic transmutation), even though the Council had previously forbidden such works.

In addition, laws were enacted due to a fear that alchemists, who believed alchemy could provide a type of divine revelation, were developing unorthodox religious positions, entering the realms of heterodoxy and dissenting views.[cclxxxv]

When it came to magic and witchcraft, the Church, although holding a dim view of it, generally didn't prosecute and its juridical processes often provided protection to people that local magistrates might not. However, in 1484, Pope Innocent VIII recognised the existence of witches in his Papal Bull, the *Summis desiderantes affectibus*. The Bull provided Papal authority for the Inquisition in Germany, under Dominican Heinrich Kramer, to prosecute witches. This was something the local ecclesiastical authorities did not support.[cclxxxvi]

By the mid-1500s, the threat of Protestantism was making the situation perilous for the Catholic Church and the climate was becoming less tolerant. The Council of Trent took place in Italy between 1545 – 1563 in order to confront this threat and, over the course of a couple of decades, it determined the Church's orthodoxies and the measures necessary to counter Protestantism, re-establishing the place of the Church within a God-given natural hierarchy.

It ruled on areas of belief that had been challenged by the Protestants, making judgements on the Sacraments; determining which were the key scriptures; agreeing issues at the heart of theological and philosophical matters around substance, the Mass and clarifying Transubstantiation - the process whereby the bread and wine change into the body and blood of Christ.

The period of the Reformation also resulted in new inquisitions, such as the Roman Inquisition. However, those in Northern Europe had much less force than some of those conducted in other regions, such as in Spain, or in earlier times. This was due to a number of factors, such as the increase in religious divisions had undermined the absolute authority of the Church to act and also that harsh punishment was found to alienate communities needed to fight in the various wars.

Instead of harsh punishment, the Church found new ways to establish its authority, such as making changes in the use of penance and the development of missions. This does not, however, mean that the wrong beliefs were treated less harshly during this time as secular, national state institutions, rather than religious ones, became the dominant authority for administering justice. It was through these that punishment and torture, particularly for serious offences, was meted out.

The Royal Courts

The royal courts of the day, like the Catholic Church, held contradictory views on alchemy.

Some were particularly receptive and provided important patronage.

The more dominant role of the Courts began to be displayed in new ways. The growing strength of the new Protestant religion and the influence of the royal courts over religious authority had resulted in a decline in the role the Church in some areas.

In contrast, the courts played a more dominant role. For example, Evans and Moran (in Nummedal 2013)[cclxxxvii] argue that the royal courts devoted substantial resources to practical alchemical projects, which might offer them some solution to the political and religious problems they encountered. Numerous courts, such as those of King James VI of Scotland[cclxxxviii] and Julius, Duke of Brunswick-Lüneburg in Germany.[cclxxxix], employed alchemists.

New entrepreneurial opportunities opened up for alchemists, many of whom were polymaths, able to work across the boundaries of different disciplines and crafts. The royal courts of Europe often employed them to develop mining and foundries and to work in areas such as medical services, chemical production, metals and gemstones.[ccxc]

Significantly, the secular court rulers hoped that the gold, resulting from the transmutation of base metals, would fill the state coffers. An alchemist's knowledge was highly valued, but there was a consequence to this new focus; a separation was opening up between the practical application of alchemy and its connection with divine knowledge.

Occult pursuits that allowed alchemists some communication with the divine order were thought to be potentially benevolent, contributing to the moral and spiritual rebirth of mankind. Alchemical practices also

> "*offered an intellectual balsam for religious and political confusion.*"[ccxci]

Yet, at the same time, there was unease around aspects of mystery and, as with the Church, witches became an issue within the royal courts. One illustration of this concern is when Henry VIII of England passed an act in 1542 making witchcraft punishable by death.[ccxcii] The focus on witches may have been caused by a fear of what might be unleased as a result of England helping initiate the Reformation. This act was repealed a few years later but new Acts were passed in 1563 and 1604.[ccxciii]

Fate also continued to be a dominant factor governing life, and by the Elizabethan period, astrology began to have a more prominent role.[ccxciv] We have already seen how John Dee used astrology to set the coronation date for Elizabeth I of England. Over in France, Nostradamus was commissioned by Catherine de' Medici to create horoscopes for her children.

Rudolf II, Holy Roman Emperor, (AD 1552 – 1612) is a very interesting character from the end of the 16th century. He re-located the Habsburg capital from

Vienna to Prague. He also hoped he could steer a middle course between Catholic and Protestant conflicts. However, his rule proved to be ineffective, and he became an isolated, secretive and reclusive figure, vainly hoping a new unity within Christendom would happen.

Despite this fairly bleak state of affairs, Rudolph drew around himself many of the great minds of the time such as Tycho Brahe and Johannes Kepler. Rudolph was a patron for the arts and culture, as well as being one of the key patrons for the development of alchemy. So, at a time when people in other parts of Europe found it dangerous to be dabbling in potentially heretical and religious practice, and could face grave consequences, Rudolph was attracting alchemists, including Dee and his associate Kelley, to his court in Prague; providing them with laboratories and allowing them to experiment.

Rudolph also created one of the best examples of a key cultural phenomena of the time, the **Kunstkammer**. A kunstkammer was a room housing notable objects - a **Cabinet of Curiosities** - seen to represent a microcosm, a world in miniature, and the Habsburg Kunstkammer was one of the best. Its aim was to be a physical encyclopedia and memory of all of nature, art, and knowledge, representing a theatre of the world and demonstrating the ruler's mastery of nature.

> *"Like many of the paintings commissioned by the Habsburg, their Kunstkammern can be read*

> *as imperial allegories, representing the ruler's symbolic mastery of the world".*[ccxcv]

Rudolf's Kunstkammer, housed in Prague Castle, was unrivalled north of the Alps; it provided solace and a retreat for contemplation[ccxcvi] that also served

> *"...to demonstrate his imperial magnificence and power in symbolic arrangement of their display..."* [ccxcvii]

Whilst his patronage may often have funded his own vanity projects, where knowledge functioned merely as a curiosity, it did allow individuals the resources and protection needed to develop new instruments and practices important for emerging scientific practice and ideas.

Over the 15th and 16th centuries Northern Europe transformed dramatically. Ultimately, the aim of the Church, to be the arbiter of truth, had failed. Hierarchy was strained.

Starting to beat a new path, a significant number of learned thinkers aimed to build on the civilisations that had gone before and started to take knowledge and thought in new directions.

CHAPTER EIGHT

THE NEW ATLANTIS to THE CITY ON THE HILL

WHEN and WHERE

AD 1572 -1712

ENGLAND • SWEDEN • GERMANY • HOLLAND • AMERICA

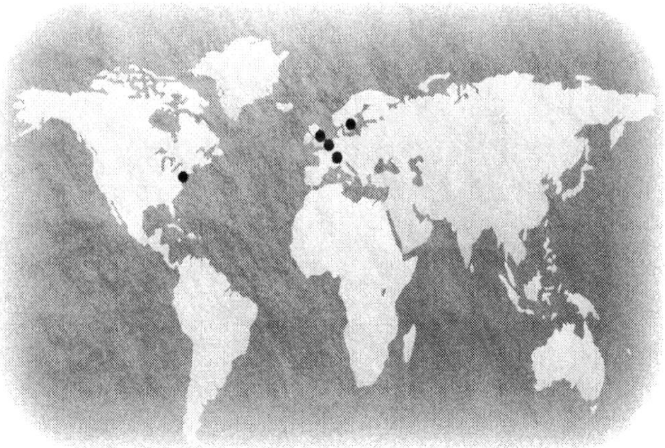

Getting your bearings

Some of the significant events that take place in the period covered in this chapter illustrate the level of conflict and change at this time. First, the murder of thousands of Huguenots by French Catholics over a few months in 1572, starting with the St. Bartholomew's Day Massacre; the Thirty Years' War 1618 and 1648; the Great Puritan Migration to the New World 1620 – 1642; the dominance of the Ottoman Empire in the East; the English Civil War of 1642 – 1646 and subsequent Glorious Revolution 1688 – 1689.

The Thirty Years' War is particularly important due to its impact on modern European development. This war, a fallout from the Reformation, was initially a religious conflict between various Protestant and Catholic states within the fragmented Holy Roman Empire. However, it developed into a more general conflict, involving most of the great powers in Europe, becoming a continuation of rivalry between France and the Habsburgs for European political pre-eminence. By its conclusion, and the signing of the Peace of Westphalia treaties (1648), Bourbon France had become established and a golden era for the Dutch was also set in motion.[ccxcviii]

Introduction

This chapter explores further the fallout from the Reformation, the shifts in power that were a consequence of this, and the experimentation that resulted from new ways of looking at the world.

Whilst the underlying thread of the last chapter was the character of man explored through the themes of lightness and darkness, this chapter examines conceptions of knowledge through mystery and reason.

Somewhat surprisingly, there is a growth in interest in alchemy, including within key institutions. This chapter describes how these major institutions adapted and changed to take account of the new ideas penetrating wider society that were making the old ways of looking at the world untenable.

Finally, this journey terminates with a brief appraisal of where this tumultuous period left questions of faith and truth.

Mystery and Reason - Staging Change

Setting the scene, a number of plays and stage dramas, written and performed at the time, illustrate much about the intellectual climate of the period.

England in the 17th century was a place where the ancient sat alongside the new, with reason, mystery and magic all combining and conflicting in new ways. The stage plays are helpful as they reflect many of the themes being explored in the later part of this book and, importantly, the seriousness and irreverence shown for some of these.

Professional theatre had become established in England in the early years of the 1600s.[ccxcix] Italian scholars had been visiting England and France since about the 1430s and communities of educated Italians living [ccc] and an increase in travel to Europe had brought Italian Renaissance theatre and humanist-influenced verse to London.

Christopher Marlow's dramatisation of the English translation of the Faust book (*The Historie of the Damnable Life and Deserved Death of Doctor John Faustus*) was published in 1604. [ccci] It includes direct references to magical practice and, significantly, turns the legend from a traditional, medieval morality play into a tragedy, and Marlow reflects this in the new title *The Tragical History of Doctor Faustus.*

In 1606, Shakespeare's *King Lear* was performed before King James VI/I [cccii.] It is a play that speaks of human nature and fate through the language of both older and contemporary philosophy, reflecting ideas of, for example, of Francis Bacon (AD 1561 – 1626) and Thomas Hobbes (AD 1588 – 1679).

In the same year, Shakespeare's *Macbeth* was also first performed. Within the play, witches loom large. The presence of The Three Witches will have been shaped by the thread of the Fates who appear throughout classical mythology. But these characters will also have been inspired by the contemporary obsessions with witches and, particularly, the paranoia of James in relation to his own fate at the hands of those believed to be able to cast spells.

In the play, the first witch claims that she set sail in a sieve, just as one of the infamous North Berwick witches was accused of doing. Additionally, the line "*Though his bark cannot be lost/Yet it shall be tempest-tossed*"[ccciii] refers to an incident from 1589 when James, bringing his new wife home to England from Denmark, was caught, and nearly lost in a storm; James believed this had been caused by a witch's curse. James introduced a new Witchcraft Act in 1604[ccciv] that included the death penalty for a first offence of raising evil spirits. [cccv]

In 1610, Ben Jonson's play, *The Alchemist*, was first performed in Oxford. The play makes fun of alchemy, illustrating the human weaknesses affecting people of all status and at all levels within society...including a satirical depiction of Puritans. The drama plays out acts of human deception, delusional dreams, fraud and the serious crime of counter-fitting.

Shakespeare's *The Tempest* was first performed before James on 'Hallowmas nyght' (1 November) 1611.[cccvi] Michael Bryson explains that magic was sometimes viewed as a force for good.

> "Prospero's fascination with his books, his being "*rapt in secret studies*" (I.ii.77), is what

> leads to his initial downfall. Prospero neglects "*all worldly ends, all dedicated / To closeness and the bettering of [his] mind*" (I.ii.89,90), thus opening the door for his usurping brother Antonio."[cccvii]

It is a many-layered tale. Prospero harnesses his magical power, not as an occult, dangerous force, but as a power he uses only temporarily, and for good ends.[cccviii]

The plays described above set the scene for the Age of Reason to come. However, during this time, there are still no clear boundaries between the objective and supernatural worlds.

The plays reflect themes relevant to the English context, but many of these would not have been out of place in most countries across Europe.

Mystery – Divine Rights, Witches and Alchemy

This section looks in more detail at how those, particularly in position of power and influence, worked within a context of a world still deeply mysterious.

Witches and The Divine Right of Kings

Across Europe, witch-trials became more common towards the end of the 1500s. The beliefs and experiences of the James VI/I helpfully illustrate the grip mystical ideas had in some parts of Europe. James, during his reign as King James VI of Scotland, contributed to the wider European discussion by writing a book on the subject, *Daemononlogie* (1597).

In some quarters there was disquiet on the use of witch trials. Over a decade before, a sceptical author, Reginal Scot, had documented his concerns in his book, *The Discoverie of Witchcraft* (1584). He brought together evidence from literature and from witch trials, showing that abnormal activity could be explained, not by witchcraft, but by trickery or some mental instability. As most of those tried were poor and uneducated, Scot saw the trials as unfair. He saw the Church as responsible for both perpetuating superstition and for acting irrationally through its prosecutions. This was at odds with his own belief that power was not in the hands of witches but lay in God. His view is called the Providential view:

> *"...it is neither a witch, nor devil, but glorious God that maketh the thunder...God maketh the blustering tempests and whirlwinds..."*[cccix]

As King of Scotland, James VI had been accustomed to exercising arbitrary powers. However, when he became King of England in 1603, he encountered an English Parliament where the rule of law was dominant and where the Court was highly intellectual and well educated. Since the Reformation, heads of state across Europe had also gained some new powers. For example, the English Act of Supremacy created a new settlement with Parliament and established a moderate Protestant Anglican Church.

However, legitimacy did not automatically come with power. The problem of establishing authority within the new state was aided by the emergence, over time, of new mythologies. One of these, the Divine Right of Kings, said the power of the King was given to him directly from God.

Once James was in England, his paranoia and superstitions shifted towards more direct threats and plots against his rule, such as he experienced from the Catholics during the gunpowder plot of 1605.

One way that James attempted to assert the Divine Right of Kings was through a campaign against witchcraft. In 1604, James extended an Elizabethan Act against witchcraft. Up until this point, this crime had been tried under ecclesiastical law, with the use of the death penalty only permitted where a person had been killed as a result of the actions of the accused. James, however, saw witchcraft not only as heresy but also as a felony. Therefore, witchcraft was to be tried, not by the clergy, but within common law, presided over by the King and punishable by death.[cccx]

However, despite the harshness of this change in the law, it was never used within England during James's reign, and even then, it seems, to have been used only once in 1645, after his reign had ended.[cccxi]

Witch-trials were, however, resurrected in the 1640s during the chaos of the English Civil War. Political conflict had resulted in a Witchfinder General, the Puritan Matthew Hopkins, being appointed and his, largely extra-parliamentary activity, was carried out mainly where the Parliamentary forces were organised - in East Anglia and in the South-East of England. Civil law had broken down[cccxii] with the law being enforced by local Justices of the Peace. Hopkins, who had been influenced by James's book *Daemonologie*, conducted a zealous campaign, resulting in the hanging of some 300 people within just the two years of 1644 and 1645.

In this new and changing context, witch trials and persecution were used mainly as a defensive weapon against the mortal threats perceived to be targeted against the King and Parliament.

There are, however, other accounts suggesting that something more complex was also taking place. For example, analysis has shown a strong relationship between a focus on witchcraft with the declining fortunes of the Catholic Church, and the rise of Protestantism and the uncertainty this created.[cccxiii]

Alternatively, as the new Protestant religion disposed of the various intermediary relationships the Church had with the congregation, the processes by which people had managed their fears of unknown forces were also removed, creating a vacuum. This vacuum was filled, in part, by the likes of Hopkins and the witch-trials.

The Secret Dissemination of Alchemy

Alongside a focus on witches and wider, dark forces, alchemical ideas were spreading throughout Europe, aided by print and by people like the German

Benedictus Figulus, publisher, alchemist and follower of Paracelsus.

However, some, like the Rosicrucian Society,[cccxiv] wanted alchemy to become even more influential and to increase the speed at which alchemical ideas were adopted.

This Rosicrucian Society had connections with influential thinkers of the late 16th and the 17th centuries such as John Dee, Robert Fludd, Elias Ashmole, Francis Bacon, Comenius, Isaac Newton, Leibniz and many others.[cccxv]

Various views and speculations developed as to why this secret group, with its esoteric knowledge, existed. One reason could have been that secrecy allowed intellectuals to preserve control over the key mystical elements of life; as protectors of esoteric, divine knowledge. Another likely reason is that the Church, with its stringent regulation of order and definition of heresies, made experimentation and the development of proto-science too risky to be practiced openly.

Reason – Senses, Utopias, Experimentation, Experience and Knowledge

Alongside the activities described above relating to those existing within the bounds of a spiritual and mystical world, many other activities we might recognise as being more rational, were proliferating. The following sections paint a picture of some of these activities.

Experience, the Senses and Certainty

Philosophers and scholars revised methodologies and changed how they viewed the earth and the heavens and the relationship between them, but this also generated many controversies and debates about proof and certainty which would, in turn, influence alchemists and their practice.

Whilst Aristotle had been a strong influence, reflections on the ancients, along with new knowledge resulting from observation, experimentation and reflection, challenged and broke, the unity of Aristotle's depiction of a harmonious universe.

We know from the previous chapter that the systematic acquisition of knowledge through observation and use of the senses had been gaining ground. This was exemplified by the outlook of Leonardo da Vinci (1452 - 1519) who had argued that truth, established from experience, must be a person's guide,

> *"If you find from your own experience that something is a fact and it contradicts what some authority has written down, then you must abandon the authority and base your reasoning on your own findings."*[cccxvi]

Another practitioner adopting an empirical approach was Vincenzo Galilei (1520 -1591), the father of Galileo. Galilei used this empirical approach during his development of musical tuning and passed this methodology on to his son.[cccxvii]

The Englishman, Francis Bacon (AD 1561 – 1626) developed an approach to the process of inquiry, requiring a systematic and methodological approach, proving significant in the development of science.

In his book *'The Advancement of Learning' (1605)* he argued that when examining the natural world, only two of Artistotle's four causes need to be considered – the *Material* and the *efficient cause.* The other two could be left to one side.

The Four Causes

The *Material* cause is the matter that makes something up
The *Formal* cause is a thing's shape or form
The *Efficient* cause creates a thing (motion)
The *Final* (first) cause is that thing's purpose

Bacon also argued that common and distinct characteristics should be isolated through a systematic application of sense perception and the nature of things drawn from the evidence derived from these observations and analysis of circumstances. This method was a forerunner to, what become known as, the scientific method.[cccxviii]

This was indeed a moment of liberation for experimentation but also a logical conclusion drawn from arguments made by Al-Razi and, later, William of Ockham, as discussed in Chapters 4 and 5. By 'putting

God aside' and focusing on the natural world, natural philosophers were free to work on their ideas unhindered, without needing to know the initial first cause or having to provide theological justifications. They also no longer needed to take account of the whole of Aristotle's complete system of thought and the complexity of his metaphysical question of *why*. The observer was also free to draw their conclusions without reference to the knowledge handed to them from some authority in the past.

Rene Descartes (AD 1596 – 1650) was another providing a challenge to Aristotle, however, grappling with existing convention and using logic, he arrived at a fresh perspective that seemed at odds with the strengthening empirical approach. Descartes disagreed with Bacon's emphasis on sense perception. The Aristotelian view held that everything that is known, first arises in the senses.[cccxix] Descartes reasoned that the senses were an unreliable guide to Truth because things can be observed differently depending on many and varied circumstances.

Drawing on his need to fundamentally question all that had gone before, Descartes sets out his argument in his Mediations (1641). He used logically reasoning and syllogism and identified one incontestable truth: a truth he believed about his mind (the unique character of the ensouled human).

> *(1) Whatever thinks exists*
> *(2) I think*

Therefore (3) I exist

Cogito, ergo sum:
I think, therefore I am,

Descartes' Cogito created a proof of Man's existence, but simultaneously, in the impalpable nature of the mind, created a proof akin to the existence of God.[cccxx] This aspect of Descartes can be seen as taking care of the two Causes, Formal and Final, left to one side by Bacon.

However, Descartes was unable to provide either a complete or coherent system,

> *"In shifting the debate from "what is true" to "of what can I be certain?", Descartes arguably shifted the authoritative guarantor of truth from God to humanity (even though Descartes himself claimed he received his visions from God)."*[cccxxi]

A Sun-Centred World - Seeing Through a New Lens

Observation was important for the age-old practice of charting the sun, planets and stars. Within a relatively short period of time, curiosity, coupled with new methods of observation and innovations, were resulting in new, profound and unsettling questions being posed concerning the substance of things, the laws governing the heavenly bodies and the extent to which these were the same or different to those governing the earth.

One early challenge was made in 1543 when Copernicus published his hypothesis asserting that the sun was at the centre of the universe. This challenged the Ptolemaic earth-centred system that had reigned since the 2nd century AD.[cccxxii]

Following Copernicus, Johannes Kepler (AD 1571 - 1630), who had been assistant to Tycho Brahe, and had drawn his own conclusions from Brahe's planetary observations, provided the first mathematical demonstration that Man does indeed inhabit a heliocentric universe and described three laws governing the motion of the planets. His first law, included in his *New Astronomy* (1609), was that the path of each planet follows the shape of an ellipse, with the Sun being one of its two foci.[cccxxiii]

Kepler's development of more sophisticated mathematics was one innovation coming from this new study of the physical world. Other innovations during this time revealed aspects of nature that the ancients had not been able to detect. For example, Galileo's lens telescope, inspired by Dutch inventions, allowed him to

> *"make out mountains and craters on the moon, as well as a ribbon of diffuse light arching across the sky — the Milky Way. He also discovered the rings of Saturn, sunspots and four of Jupiter's moons."*[cccxxiv]

Newton (AD 1642 - 1727), inspired by people such as Kepler and Galileo, developed a law of universal gravitation, indicating relationships between particles, developing an understanding of a world through a use of mathematics [cccxxv] and applying new, abstract conceptions such as mass.[cccxxvi] These advances created new perspectives and raised important questions forcing a reconsideration of past assumptions.

The discoveries that were revealing the workings of nature, presented a new set of contradictions. A new, mechanical world view reduced the traditional role of God,[cccxxvii] Uzgalis (2018) says,

> *"...Newton recognized the essential fact that remains at the core of modern science with its material explanations for physical events. In a world composed entirely of matter in motion, the traditional role of God had to shrink. The author of a mechanical universe could put events in train, but after that primary impulse, the cosmos could then wend its way forward through time on its own."*[cccxxviii]

Intellectual Circles and Universal Knowledge

Indicating how the balance of ideas was shifting in new ways, there was a mushrooming of intellectual circles exploring and debating the wide range of profound questions being asked. Furthermore, these circles also provided the means through which experiments could be conducted. A couple of examples below illustrate the range of activity being undertaken, within which alchemists played an active part.

The Invisible College - focused on experiment and is seen as a forerunner to the *Royal Society of London.* The group, consisting of several natural philosophers, including the influential chemist Robert Boyle, met

> "*...to acquire knowledge through experimental investigation*".[cccxxix]

The concept of such a college is mentioned in a few places in the early 1600s, including the German Rosicrucian pamphlets and by Ben Johnson in relation to Bacon's Solomon's House.[cccxxx]

Salons – an example of a salon is the one organised by Lady Katherine Ranelagh, Boyle's sister which took place during the 1650s at her London house, complete with a laboratory. This salon was frequented by specialists and virtuosi in various fields and associated with Samuel Hartlib.[cccxxxi]

Other groups included the *Académie Parisienne, The Hartlib Circle, The Great Tew Circle* and, importantly, *The Royal Society.* Many of the individuals within the intellectual circles were linked to the secretive Rosicrucian Society.

A number of key individuals, orbiting around The Royal Society, tried to influence the ways knowledge was to be created and propagated. For example, German-British polymath, Samuel Hartlib (AD 1600 – 1662), attempted to promote a closed, hermetic, utopian fellowship based on a rigid brand of Christian socialism, portrayed by Johann Valentin Andreae's concept of a Brotherhood, in his utopian tract, *Christianopolis.*[cccxxxii]

In comparison, Francis Bacon, who was more interested in reform of the natural sciences created a utopian vision, called the **New Atlantis**, underpinned by his vision that reform would bring about a purified religion and a revitalised natural philosophy. In his utopian ideal city, he depicts the Bensalem's school of natural philosophy as the House of Solomon. This school would investigate nature in a reverent attempt to discover the benefits a loving God placed in creation.[cccxxxiii]

The Golden Age of Alchemy

Within these thriving intellectual communities, the practice of alchemy, although shrouded in secrecy, also grew in strength, becoming *the golden age of alchemy.* The following section includes a rich picture of the alchemists at work.

In terms of the emerging new culture of intellectual ideas, the court of Christina of Sweden is important at this point due to its patronage of philosophy, science and the arts. Christina exemplified the contradiction in ideas of the time. She displayed the new rationality of the period by employing Descartes, albeit temporarily, as her tutor. But she was also influenced by alchemy and, later in life, she turned to Catholicism.

Alchemy was embedded in experimental practice and, proto chemistry, one way to understand alchemy, developed through the work of some of the following individuals.

Michael Sendivogius (AD 1566–1636) a Polish, pioneering chemist, and possibly a spy for Rudolph II investigating alchemical practices taking place in other royal courts,[cccxxxiv] developed methods of purification and creation of acids, metals and other chemical compounds. One hundred years before Scheele's discovery of Oxygen, Sendivogius discovered that air is not a single substance and that it contained within it a life-giving substance.

Johann Rudolf Glauber (AD 1604 - 1670) a German-Dutch alchemist and perhaps the first chemical engineer. He was known for his "Glauber's Salt" and paved the way for gold ruby glass.[cccxxxv]

Eirenaeus Philalethes (George Starkey) (AD 1628 - 1665) from Bermuda in the New World. He studied at Harvard and was a Colonial American alchemist, medical practitioner, and writer of numerous commentaries and chemical treatises widely circulated in Europe. His methodology and practice influenced prominent men of science, including Robert Boyle, whom he tutored, and Isaac Newton.[cccxxxvi]

Hennig Brand (AD 1630 - 1710) was a German alchemist and discoverer of Phosphorus from urine.

And Johann Conrad Dippel (AD 1673 - 1734), born in the legendary Frankenstein Castle, Mühltal, in Germany, contributed to the invention of the pigment

Prussian Blue. Given his passion for dissecting animals, he could have been a source of inspiration for Mary Shelley's Dr Frankenstein in her book *Frankenstein Or, The Modern Prometheus.*

Manufacture was another area of experimentation.

Johann Friedrich Böttger (AD 1682 – 1719) a German alchemist. He was instructed by King Frederick I of Prussia to produce gold from base metal. His legacy is more normally associated with being one of the first Europeans to discover how to create hard-paste porcelain, achieved in 1708.[cccxxxvii]

In the area of new technological breakthroughs and advances in methods of experimentation.

Cornelis Drebbel (AD 1572 – 1633) a Dutch engineer, inventor, engraver and alchemist who created continuous mobile machines and the first navigable submarine in 1620. He developed red dye, measurement and control systems and optics.[cccxxxviii]

Johann Joachim Becher (AD 1635 – 1682) was a German physician, alchemist and advocated a method of state-controlled economy (cameralism) that was adopted in Austria. He also formulated the Phlogiston theory to explain both combustion and rusting.

Isaac Newton (AD 1642 – 1727) whilst making fundamental breakthroughs in science also took alchemy extremely seriously. It seems that he and John Locke had some literary exchanges on the topic, aimed at identifying how to create the Philosopher's Stone and how to use the work Robert Boyle had developed in this area.[cccxxxix]

Newton was a committed alchemist, and over a thirty-year period, he wrote about a million words on the topic as well as reading and experimenting within this practice.[cccxl]

Levenson suggests that Newton hoped to discover,

> *"...the method God used to produce gold from base mixtures and if he succeeded then he would know – and not just believe – that the King of Kings would indeed reign triumphant, forever and ever."*[cccxli]

The examples above illustrate the prevalence of the practice of alchemy. Experimentation required using the known to find the unknown, using observation to witness the new and using mystery to discover truth. It required hours and hours of patience, of weighing and measuring and, for many including Newton, it ended in failure.

The Case, Again, for Universal Knowledge

The systematic and rigorous approach to acquiring, categorising and indexing knowledge reflected a wider aspiration echoing Alexandrian Hellenism - the creation of a single body of knowledge. The next sections on libraries, classification and the encyclopaedia are useful as they underscore that the intellectual community was moving in a direction where knowledge was documented, classified and, over time, organised within understandable categories with relationships between subject areas considered. Ultimately this would become the source of universal knowledge.

A Rebirth of Libraries – and Re-establishing the Collecting Habit

Over the entrance to the library at Wolfenbüttel, Germany, a golden, Latin instruction said:

> *"If [the reader] finds anything not entirely to his taste, or something in his view too strongly to be approved, let him contain himself calmly and reflect on it in silence..."*[cccxlii]

This was a period of mixed fortunes for libraries.

During the Reformation and then later, during the Thirty Years War, many libraries had been closed, falling into disrepair, or their books destroyed or taken as booty.

It is a profound and deep irony that the collection and transportation of intellectual ideas to Northern Europe, initiated mainly by the Church to establish its own authority by way of the Truth, ended with the destruction of these books and their ancient storehouses due to conflict between religious and secular powers.

England, for example, dismantled or destroyed its historic monastic libraries following the Act of

Succession in 1534. The dissolution of the monasteries brought about the dismantling of 900 religious houses. Although alternative storehouses were set up for some of the books and manuscripts that had been removed, only a few of the texts, from the many hundreds dispersed across the land, were retained. For example, of the 600 books taken from Worcester Priory (now Worcester Cathedral), only 6 are known to have survived. And of the 646 volumes of books at the abbey of the Augustinian Friars in York, only 3 are known to be survivors of this period[cccxliii]. A few collections at Cathedral libraries, such as the one in Durham, managed to stay largely intact.

A new momentum behind library development and book collection did however begin again. Some libraries were, as in the past, created for the status these provided, such as the development of the Bavarian State Library in Munich. Some princes had a deeper, more personal interest. The Duke Augustus of Brunswick-Luneburg (AD 1579 – 1666) inherited, then expanded, the library of the ruling family, mainly paid for from his own money. He wrote his own detailed catalogue and cross-referencing. He opened his library for use by people including ecclesiastical and lay councillors.

<u>Christina of Sweden</u> created both a library and laboratory within her residence. She didn't shy away from taking books as war booty, removing the

significant collection of treasures from Rudolph IIs Kunstkammer in 1648 (as described in chapter 7).

Some older libraries, such as the library at Oxford University, gained a new lease of life, becoming a feature of the university. The Bodleian Library, opening in 1602, and made from mainly private donations, was primarily a collection of Protestant theology used by graduates and Lords, although texts from other doctrines were kept and could be accessed on request, including by the public. Trinity College, Dublin, having established itself "*...as a centre of the Protestant religion and English manners in Ireland*"[cccxliv], held another major collection. The Archbishop of Armagh, who previously owned this collection, held many manuscripts relating to ecclesiastical biblical criticism, many having belonged to monasteries before the dissolution. He had also held texts supplied by merchants from the Levant including heretical scientific and religious texts. These all kept him informed of recent studies and developments. [cccxlv]

Compared to the old monastic libraries, these new ones had different reasons for existing. Some were more specialist whilst others became more diverse, serving a wider audience. Some began employing intellectual scholars with the capability and status to manage significant collections. For example, the philosopher and mathematician, Leibniz became Chief Librarian at Wolfenbüttel from 1690 to 1716, followed then by the Enlightenment thinker Gotthold Lessing.[cccxlvi]

One collection that indicated the dramatic change in collections was the library of Samuel Pepys.[cccxlvii] Its content was wide-ranging and vast, including texts relating to naval matters, heretical texts, works of literature, science, poetry, music, prints and maps. The collection encompassed both modern and new learning, no longer restricted to the authoritative sources of old. Pepys's collection shows that Europe was letting go of its Renaissance-inspired past, creating a new world view with new forms of knowledge.[cccxlviii]

Classification

Linked to the enterprise of gathering knowledge within libraries was the 17th century development of advanced classification systems to arrange and manage these collections.

Francis Bacon, an important patron of libraries, assisted with this task of developing a system, applying three functional categories – History, Poetry and Philosophy. These categories were devised to be broad enough to ensure that knowledge, yet to be discovered, could be incorporated in the future. Bacon set forth his idea for reforming the entire realm of knowledge in *The Proficience and Advancement of Learning Divine and Human* (1605).[cccxlix]

Locke contributed to the conceptual idea of knowledge classification in his *An Essay on Human Understanding* (1690). Locke noted the importance of abstract, general ideas, as these serve knowledge as 'sorts' under which all the vast multitude of particular existences can be ranked. Summarising his method, Uzgalis (2018) says:

> *"Thus, abstract ideas and classification are of central importance in Locke's discussion of language and its importance for knowledge. Without general terms and classes we would be faced with the impossible task of trying to know a vast world of particulars."*[cccl]

The Encyclopaedia

Along with libraries and the project of classification, the encyclopaedia became a prominent tool in natural science; encompassing the idea of universal knowledge. Sir Thomas Browne used the word 'encyclopaedia' in 1646, defining his *Pseudodoxia Epidemica*, a major work of the 17th-century scientific revolution. Browne structured his encyclopaedia around the Renaissance scheme. This 'scale of creation' ascends through the mineral, vegetable, animal, human, planetary, and cosmological worlds.[cccli]

Another person developing the concept of the encyclopedia was the educational innovator John Amos Comenius (AD 1592 – 1670), considered to be the father of modern education.[ccclii]. He shared the Baconian belief in the possibility of universal knowledge which he thought could be achieved through the synthesis of all knowledge into a harmonious whole.[cccliii] He also strove towards panosophia, the idea that all this knowledge should be taught to everyone.[cccliv] His optimistic belief in human capacity is reflected in his idea for the development of a pansophic movement[ccclv] that would bring all this knowledge within the grasp of every child[ccclvi]. He prototyped new forms of picture-based books that would stimulate reading and observation. One example was his picture book, *Orbis Sensualium Pictus*, (The World of Things Obvious to the Senses, 1658). In this book the student asks,

> *"What doth this mean, to be wise?"* And his teacher answers, *"To understand rightly, to do rightly, and to speak out rightly all that are necessary."*[ccclvii]

Despite the efforts to create this comprehensive, encyclopaedic knowledge, it became clear over time that this was not humanly possible. Paul Heidebrecht (1987) suggests that instead, there was a more modest function. Encyclopaedic knowledge,

> *"...implied a way of organizing the facts of knowledge, so they would express wisdom and constitute knowledge of practical utility."*[ccclviii]

Both Bacon and Comenius shared this vision of an orderly structure of knowledge and carried forward the effort to place it upon a scientific foundation, superseding Renaissance thinking.

Language and Arabic Studies

The chapter on Italian Humanism showed how the reintroduction of Platonic and Eastern ideas shaped some aspects of Western thinking. Another example of Eastern influences comes from within England.

Archbishop William Laud (1573 – 1645), also Chancellor of the University of Oxford, recognised the significant role the Arabs had played in acting as custodians of ancient texts.[cccllix] He created and funded a position of Chair of Arabic at Oxford in 1636, which he offered to Edward Pococke, clergyman and the foremost Arabist of the time. Pococke, learnt Arabic and other languages including Greek and Hebrew. He went to Aleppo (now in Syria) in the 1630s where he served as Chaplain to the Levant Company.

Following Lauds request, Pococke returned to England, carrying both coins and oriental manuscripts, and became the first professor of Arabic at the university.[ccclx] Laud arranged it so that every ship belonging to the Levant Company must carry at least one manuscript back with them when returning to an English port.[ccclxi]

As a brief reminder to us that these were dangerous times, not open and liberal, Laud was beheaded for Treason at Towerhill in 1645 for his perceived role in stirring conflict between the Crown and Puritan Parliament through his efforts to retain, for example, the more traditional, intermediary role of the priest in ritual.

Travel and The Grand Tour

The Grand Tour was another activity marking a shift towards empirical thinking. Travel became a necessary part of how knowledge needed to be gained as direct observation was required. Although nearly every scholar, academic and philosopher referred to throughout these chapters spent extended periods travelling, and sometimes working, in several countries, travel now became emblematic of a modern world.

Crichton-Miller (2016)[ccclxii], suggests that it was the architect Inigo Jones, embarking on a tour of Europe with the young Earl of Arundel in 1613, who set the pattern of The Grand Tour, which continued for more than 200 years. Jones and Arundel passed through France, Switzerland and Italy, down to Naples, seeking out artists and studying both ancient Roman and Renaissance architecture. The Earl became a prodigious collector of antiques and Renaissance and contemporary art. Jones was appointed Surveyor of the King's Works, transforming architecture and building a series of astonishing neoclassical buildings, including the Queen's House, Greenwich, and the Banqueting House, Whitehall.

The Grand Tour was adopted by those wanting to, or feeling obliged to, be associated with this new approach. Buzard (2002) says,

> *"Following the great Renaissance age of colonial exploration and expansion, an articulated, systematic empiricism made travelling about the world and seeing the new and different 'something like an obligation for the person conscientious about developing the mind and accumulating knowledge'."*[ccclxiii]

This chapter has, so far, drawn up a balance sheet of some of the different ways people thought about their world during the late 1500s and during the 1600s. The many activities described illustrate that there was no clear-cut boundary or separation between rational and irrational ideas but there had, undoubtedly, been a move away from the theoretic approach towards one where gathering information through experience and observation was far more central.

The Limits of Knowledge

This last section looks at the discussion again, but through the work of a key thinker of this period, **John Locke** (AD 1632 – 1704), an English philosopher and physician.

His *An Essay Concerning Human Understanding* (1690), not written until the end of the tumultuous 1600s, and towards the latter part of Locke's life was about knowledge. Locke wanted to understand thought in a unified way, not compartmentalised like Bacon. He wanted to understand how we know and where knowledge comes from. His text became one of the principal sources influencing empiricism in modern Western philosophy.

Locke systematically examined the process by which knowledge is gained, exploring the processes and actions the mind undertakes to make sense of experience. His reflections suggested that men were looking at the problem from the wrong end. Locke introduced a new dimension to the Faustian tragedy as he thought Men believed they could answer questions by throwing themselves into the "*boundless extent*"[ccclxiv] of our being, without prior consideration of what it was and wasn't possible for Men to know.

Locke also explored where knowledge came from. In this he was influenced by the wealth of ideas that surround him but also by a particular book - Ibn Tufail's (c. 1105 – 1185) story, *Hayy ibn Yaqdhan* now associated with the class of utopian texts mentioned earlier. This book came to Locke's attention because it had been translated from Arabic to Latin in 1671 by Edward Pococke the younger, tutor of Locke (Pococke changing the name of the book to *Philosophus Autodidactus*).[ccclxv]

The focus of the story is on how Hayy gains knowledge from experience, and this was an idea that was significant for Locke. In Locke's Essay, he tests the idea of a *priori* knowledge and whether we start our life with or without knowledge, concluding it to be the latter.

Summarising a key aspect of Locke's approach, Uzgalis (2018) says,

> *"Locke, like Descartes, is tearing down the foundations of the old Aristotelian scholastic house of knowledge. But while Descartes focused on the empiricism at the foundation of the structure, Locke is focusing on the claims that innate ideas provide its first principles. The attack on innate ideas is thus the first step in the*

> *demolition of the scholastic model of science and knowledge."*[ccclxvi]

This chapter has provided an account of this period which includes the golden age of alchemy. On balance, the material indicates that the side of 'reason' gained the upper hand through the adoption of a more systematic, empirical approach, using experimentation and observation combined with a process for categorising and classifying the natural world.

However, it is also the case that the notions of reason and mystery remained intertwined, with a clear line between them still not being entirely evident.

Contradictions of Faith – Establishing Truth

So where, within this balance sheet of mystery and reason, does this leave the question of faith? And was gaining Truth possible?

Most of the people making the great leaps forward in invention or discovery were devout believers and wished to repel the opinions of detractors who tried to suggest otherwise.

Francis Bacon was a devout Anglican. In his *Essays, Civil and Moral*, published in 1597, he affirms that,

> *"...a little philosophy inclineth man's mind to atheism*[3] *but depth in philosophy bringeth men's minds about to religion.*"[ccclxvii ccclxviii]

[3] Atheism meant more than a lack of belief in God – it also

Robert Boyle argued in his book, *Disquisition About the Final Causes of Natural Things* (1688), that the inquiry by natural philosophers into areas where design was apparently on display, would reveal Gods involvement with the world.[ccclxix]

Similarly, Newton thought that the ordered complexity of the universe provided new evidence verifying God's existence, as only God could create such an ordered and complex thing.

These great thinkers hoped to find new demonstrations of God's existence and used alchemy, for example, to do this.

However, for some, pursuing this practice appeared to be a hopeless miscalculation. Newton's biographer, Sir David Brewster, writing in the mid-1800s, believed Newton's investigations into alchemy were irrational and a wasted effort. Whilst expressing his incredulity at Newton's interest in this area, Brewster also felt he should make some allowances, believing that Newton's misplaced investigations were, fundamentally, motivated by a love of truth,

> *"But we cannot understand how a mind of such power [as Newton's]...could stoop to be even the copyist of the most contemptible alchemical poetry, and the annotator of a work, the obvious production of a fool and a knave."* [ccclxx]

---

implied anarchy

Cambridge scholar Simon Schaffer provided a contrasting view on Newton's investigations into alchemy. In his 1984 documentary about this scientist, Schaffer speculated that Newton was trying to retrieve knowledge from ancient alchemical texts; digging into things society didn't understand, namely, the active power in matter which he believed was manifest in gravity.[cclxxi]

It is, to some extent, counter-intuitive for our contemporary mind, that as some of the workings of nature only became better understood because the desire to know God meant they refused the advice of Erasmus to only "*..look in awe and with simple faith on whatever it is that is concealed from you.*" Newton believed, like Boyle and Locke, that alchemy could be used to find out what was concealed. In examining the frenzied laboratory notes made by Newton during an intense period of secretive research, Levenson states that Newton believed,

> "*...he found the stone of the ancients; an imitation of God's will in the world. It was the moment when Newton, and Newton alone, peered into the mechanism of divine action this side of heaven.*"[cclxxii]

Newton believed that he would find life's force. The idea that existence might be reduced to a Cartesian, mechanistic, soulless process was not something that he could contemplate. However, whilst form, substance, motion, gravity, space etc, revealed themselves, The Divine remained elusive.

Knowledge and Tolerance

At the end of the golden age of alchemy, Locke held, like many others, contradictory ideas.

Faith in God remained. But as Locke argued in his *Essay on Human Understanding,* this could only be arrived at through an individual's own rational thought and personal faith. He argued that it was not legitimate to assert without proof that others must hold the same faith as one's own,

> "...*he that takes away Reason to make way for Revelation, puts out the Light of both, and does much the same, as if he would perswade a Man to put out his eyes, the better to receive the remote Light of an invisible Star by a Telescope.*" *(IV.19.4, N: 698)*

The Englishman and Puritan, Samuel Danforth, (AD 1626 – 1674) in contrast to Locke, exemplified the intolerance of the age; unable to grant that others shared his own capacity for reason. His family, moving to New England was part of the Puritan settlement. At this time, the leader of the Massachusetts Bay Colony John Winthrop, hoped this new community would become a new utopia, an ideal city modelled on the Christian City on the Hill described in Jesus's Sermon on the Mount.

Danforth, in keeping with this Puritan outlook, used the occasion of the appearance of a comet in 1664, to warn the people of New England that they were falling away from their divine mission. His account of the comet appeared in a book he wrote, one of the first works of astronomy printed in America.[ccclxxiii]

To counter this failing of the community, he promoted a general reformation of morals. The religious, moral control of the Puritans continued, resulting in members of the community being made examples of, with one of these being executed in 1674 (see also Samuel Danforth's execution speech[ccclxxiv]). Furthermore, these actions only engendered fear and hysteria rather than faith. It is within Massachusetts between 1692 and 1693 that the Salem Witch Trials took place.

And what became of alchemy? It seems that it was only when the more formal discipline of science developed, and the high point of alchemy's golden age had passed, that alchemical works were more widely published and readily available. *The Aphorismi Urbigerani* of 1690, produced by Baru Urbigerus (AD 1626 – 1689), claims to set out the complete theory of the alchemical work and the preparation of the Philosopher's Stone. But it is likely that making such a work available was only possible once interest in using alchemy for attaining divine knowledge had declined as a practice, allowing its 'secrets' to be given up more easily.

Some mythology around alchemy persisted, such as

around the French enigmatic Count of St. Germain (AD 1712). But those interested in alchemy, such as the Frenchman Fulcanelli, and his student Caseliet, or the American husband and wife alchemy team Richard and Isabella Ingalese, were now much more peripheral figures to the discussions that were now taking place.

REFLECTIONS AND CONCLUSIONS

Alchemy: A Search for Truth. What was the Truth being searched for? And, given no one had made gold, was there any value in this effort?

The answer to these questions lies in the dual nature of the practice of alchemy.

Using experimental processes, alchemists aimed to discover the Truth within nature that would allow the transmutation of base metals into their higher, noble forms. Second, through this process, alchemists also hoped to gain a greater, underlying Truth which was knowledge of the Divine. In this sense, alchemy failed. It failed to change base metals to gold and therefore it also failed to find the secrets of nature and Divinity.

However, I think the story of alchemy shows that the search for Truth was about making sense of the world, by making meaning from the knowledge that was gained. And, although it fell short of what had been craved for, knowledge was gained and compromises around unanswered questions were made with the development of orthodoxies often being an admission of this compromise.

When reflecting back on the different people covered throughout this book, it seems that those living, for example, during the golden age of alchemy in the 16th and 17th centuries experienced a problem shared, to some extent, by those in Mesopotamia around 300 BC.

They shared a problem of the gap between knowledge and meaning.

Babylonian farmers were left behind when their priests started setting calendars one hundred years in advance. The priest's expertise in charting of the heavens was of little relevance to those whose life was shaped by the seasons and annual crop production and who felt estranged from the new celestial gods that emerged.

In the golden age of alchemy, it was the priests, however, who were left behind. The ground-breaking astronomers broke the Aristotelian system, with its inner and continuous harmony of an unchanging hierarchical world, ruled by the stars. They filled this space with a new spirit connecting the heavens and the earth. It was the old world that no longer made sense to the wider population and a new spirit seemed within people's direct grasp.

In the golden age of alchemy, an abundance of new knowledge was gained but meaning was harder to arrive at. Alchemy, from today's perspective, holds little meaning. But it provides a useful way to think about Truth.

Hannah Arendt, discussing the *Life of the Mind* (1977 – 78) and the impact the unquenchable search for knowledge has on us, makes the point that,

> *"...the activity itself leaves behind a growing treasure of knowledge that is retained and kept*

> *in store by every civilization as part and parcel of its world."*[i]

Animating this phenomena, each of the chapter headings of this book, starting with the House of Life and ending at the City on the Hill, illustrate how different civilisations have achieved this. Whilst the knowledge in these stores might have been partial truths, each of the societies owning these treasures made common sense meaning from their knowledge.

Turning to a different kind of truth, where the intellect necessarily leaves one out on a limb, straining to know an objective truth, Arendt points out that this,

> "*...leaves nothing so tangible behind, and the need to think can therefore never be stilled by the insights of "wise men".*[ii]

Whether within Locke's **boundless extent of our being** or Erasmus's ***impia curiositas,*** the limits to knowledge have been policed by the defenders of orthodoxy and breached by heretics, the latter finding the systems that had been created to explain the world no longer made sense or provided meaning.

However, within this shifting terrain, there was a successful transmutation taking place, but it was not of base metals but within the minds of Men, using their ingenuity and ever-expanding imagination.

This unshakable curiosity did not burn out with the end of golden age of alchemy but, instead, continued on, next stop, the *Vitalist* movement of the 18th and 19th centuries.

A concept backed by the Royal College of Surgeons, *Vitalism* hoped to find, like a version of the elixir of life, the spark of life. Providing a kind of afterword to the story of the journey of alchemy, Mary Shelley's *Frankenstein Or, The Modern Prometheus* posed again the question of whether going beyond the boundaries – as Dedalus, Icarus, Bruno and Faust had done - demonstrated hubris or Man's true humanity.

> *"With an anxiety that almost amounted to agony, I collected the instruments of life around me, that I might infuse a spark of being into the lifeless thing that lay at my feet."*[iii]

The legacy of the Search for Truth is the need to continually identify the new boundaries and limits, whether on the earth or in the skies, that the marshals of orthodoxy have taped off. Where next…?

HISTORY OF ALCHEMY PODCAST EPISODES FEATURED

http://www.podcastnik.com/history-of-alchemy-podcast

Text underlined within the book = a History of Alchemy series episode

Terms	
Hermeticism	Theurgy
Philosopher's stone	
Alchemists	
Ostanes	Heinrich Khunrath
Agathodaimaon	Paracelsus
Miriam the Jewess	Alexander Von Suchten
Pseudo-Democritus	John Dee
Zosimos of Panopolis	Elizabeth I
Khalid ibn Yazid (Calid)	Edward Kelley
Jabir ibn Hayyan (Geber)	Robert Fludd
Al-Razi	Basil Valentine
Al-Ghazali	Giovanni Agostino Panteo
Maslama al-Majriti	Rudolf II, Holy Roman Emperor
Albertus Magnus	Benedictus Figulus
Thomas Aquinas	Christina of Sweden
Roger Bacon	Michael Sendivogius
Ramon Llull	Johann Rudolf Glauber
Paul of Taranto	Eirenaeus Philalethes (George Starkey)
Pico della Mirandola	Hennig Brand
Francesco Giorgi	Johann Conrad Dippel
Giovanni (Mercurio) da Corregio	Johann Friedrich Böttger
Peter Bonus	Cornelis Drebbel
Nicolas Flamel	Johann Joachim Becher
Bernard Trevisan	Isaac Newton

Podcast Episodes

Gilles de Rais	Samuel Danforth
Albert the Great	Baru Urbigerus
Tycho Brahe	Count of St. Germain
Henry Cornelius Agrippa	Richard and Isabella Ingalese

CHAPTER NOTES: RESOURCES, BIBLIOGRAPHY AND REFERENCES

Resources

Alchemy

History of Alchemy podcast

https://www.podcastnik.com/history-of-alchemy-podcast

Alchemy website

https://www.alchemywebsite.com/index.html

Society for the History of Alchemy & Chemistry

https://www.ambix.org/

Other key references sites

The Stanford Encyclopedia of Philosophy

https://plato.stanford.edu/

The Internet Encyclopedia of Philosophy (IEP)

https://www.iep.utm.edu/

History of Philosophy Without any Gaps

https://historyofphilosophy.net/home

Philosophy Now

https://philosophynow.org/

Encyclopaedia Britannica

https://www.britannica.com/

Wikipedia

https://en.wikipedia.org/wiki/Main_Page

Literature and History podcast

https://literatureandhistory.com/

The Internet Classics Archive

http://classics.mit.edu/index.html

Ancient History Encyclopaedia

https://www.ancient.eu/
In our time
https://www.bbc.co.uk/programmes/b006qykl
The New Atlantis
https://www.thenewatlantis.com/
Science History Institute
https://www.sciencehistory.org/
History of Information
http://www.historyofinformation.com/

Bibliography

Adamson, P. & Taylor, R.C. (2005) *The Cambridge Companion to Arabic Philosophy*, Cambridge University Press.

Al-Khalili, J. (2012) *The House of Wisdom: How Arabic Science Saved Ancient Knowledge and Gave Us the Renaissance.* Penguin Books

Arendt, H. (1981) The life of the Mind. Vols 1 & 2. Harvest/HBJ Book

Armstrong, A.H. (1989) *An Introduction to Ancient Philosophy.* Rowman & Littlefield.

Barzun, J. (2000). *From Dawn to Decadence: 500 Years of Western Cultural Life.* Harper Collins

Birch, D. and Hooper, K. (Ed) 30 May 2013. *The Concise Oxford Companion to English Literature.* OUP Oxford

Bottéro, J and Bahrani, Z. (June 1995) Mesopotamia: Writing, Reasoning, and the Gods. University of Chicago Press.

Brewster, D, Sir (1855) *Memoirs of the life, writings, and discoveries of Sir Isaac Newton.* Edinburgh, T. Constable and Co.

Burns, R. (2005) *Damascus: A History.* Psychology Press.

Butler, E.M. (1952) *The fortunes of Faust*. Cambridge University Press

Buzard, J. (2002). *The Grand Tour and after* (1660-1840). In P. Hulme & T. Youngs (Eds.), The Cambridge Companion to Travel Writing (Cambridge Companions to Literature, pp. 37-52). Cambridge: Cambridge University Press

Carpi,D; Leiboff, M; de Gruyter, W. (2016) *Fables of the Law: Fairy Tales in a Legal Context*. GmbH & Co KG, 24 Oct 2016 p. 98 -101

Cobb, C. and Goldwhite, H. (2002) Creations of Fire: Chemistry's Lively History from Alchemy to the Atomic Age. Basic Books

D'Acona, C. (2005) *Chp 2. Greek into Arabic: Neoplatonism in translation* in Adamson, P. and Taylor,R.C. (2005) The Cambridge Companion to Arabic Philosophy. Cambridge University Press.

Cantor, N.F. (1993). *The Civilization of the Middle Ages: a completely revised and expanded edition of Medieval history, the life and death of a civilization*. HarperCollins

Dunand, F. and Zivie-Coche,C. (2004) Gods and men in Egypt: 3000 BCE to 395 CE. Ithaca, NY: Cornell University Press. Source

Durant, W. (1953) *The Renaissance. The Story of Civilization*. New York: Simon and Schuster.

Ebenstein, Alan; William Ebenstein (2002) *Introduction to Political Thinkers*. Wadsworth Group.

Eberly, J. (2005) *Al-Kimia: The Mystical Islamic Essence of the Sacred Art of Alchemy*. Sophia Perennis.

Evans, G.R. (2010) *The University of Oxford: A New History*. I B Tauris & Co Ltd; 1st edn edition

Fakhry, M. *A History of Islamic Philosophy:* Third Edition, Columbia University Press (2004)

Furedi, F. (2013) Authority: A sociological history. Cambridge University Press

Garvey, J. and Stangroom, J. (2012) *The Story of Philosophy: A History of Western Thought*. Quercus.

Goodrick-Clarke, N. (2008) The Western Esoteric Traditions: A Historical Introduction. Oxford Uni Press

Gutas, D. (1998) *Greek Thought, Arabic Culture: The Graeco-Arabic Translation Movement in Baghdad and Early 'Abbasaid Society*. Routledge

Harris, M. (1999) *History of Libraries in the Western World* The Scarecrow Press, Inc.; 4 edition (29 July 1999) 4th ed

Hoyland, R.G. (2014) *In God's Path: The Arab Conquests and the Creation of an Islamic Empire.* Oxford University Press

Kilgour, Frederick G. (1998) *The Evolution of the Book.* School of Library and Information Sciences Frederick G Kilgour Oxford University Press.

König, J., Oikonomopoulou, K. and Woolf, G. (2016) *Ancient Libraries*

Lapidus, I.M. (2014) *A History of Islamic Societies*: Third Edition. Cambridge University Press.

Lindberg, David C. (1992). *The beginnings of Western Science: The European scientific tradition in philosophical, religious, and institutional context, prehistory to AD 1450.* University of Chicago Press 2nd edition 2007

Lyons, Jonathan (2009), *The House of Wisdom: How the Arabs Transformed Western Civilization*, New York: Bloomsbury Press.

Malik, K. (2014) *The Quest for a Moral Compass*. Atlantic Books.

Findlen, P. (ed) (2002) *Merchants and Marvels: Commerce, Science, and Art in Early Modern Europe*. Routledge.

Furedi, F. (2013) *Authority: A sociological history.* Cambridge University Press.

Hart, G., (2005) *The Routledge Dictionary of Egyptian Gods and Goddesses.* Routledge, second edition, Oxon

Hadot, P. (1995) Philosophy as a Way of Life: Spiritual Exercises from Socrates to Foucault. Davidson, A. (Editor) Wiley-Blackwell.

Hobson, A. (1979) *Great Libraries.* D.H. Greaves Ltd

Janacek, B. (2011) *Alchemical Belief Occultism in the Religious Culture of Early Modern England.* Penn State Press

Kilgour, Frederick G. (1998) *The Evolution of the Book.* School of Library and Information Sciences Frederick G Kilgour Oxford University Press

Kusukawa, S. (1996). *Bacon's classification of knowledge.* In M. Peltonen (Ed.), The Cambridge Companion to Bacon (Cambridge Companions to Philosophy, pp. 47-74). Cambridge University Press

Leroi, A.M. (2015) *The Lagoon: How Aristotle Invented Science.* Bloomsbury

Levenson. T. (2009) *Newton and the counterfeiter.* Faber & Faber

Carpi,D; Leiboff, M; de Gruyter, W. (2016) *Fables of the Law: Fairy Tales in a Legal Context*. GmbH & Co KG, 24 Oct 2016 p. 98 -101

Olsen, R. (1982) Science deified and science defied: The historical significance of science in Western Culture. University of California Press

Newman. Willian, R. (2005) *Promethean Ambitions: Alchemy and the Quest to Perfect Nature.* Chicago University Press.

Principe, Lawrence M. (2012) *The secrets of alchemy.* University of Chicago Press

Riedweg, C. (2005) [2002] *Pythagoras: His Life, Teachings, and Influence,* Ithaca, New York: Cornell University Press

Ring, T; Salkin, Robert, M; Berney, KA; Schellinger, P.E. eds. (1994). International dictionary of historic places. Chicago.

Robin, D. (2007) *Publishing Women: Salons, The Presses, and the counter-reformation in sixteenth-century Italy.* University Chicago Press.
Russell, B. (1946) History of Western Philosophy. p.236. Routledge.
Russell, G. A. (1994), *The 'Arabick' Interest of the Natural Philosophers in Seventeenth-Century England.* Brill Publishers
Ryholt, K. (2016) *Libraries in ancient Egypt* Eds. König, J., Oikonomopoulou, K. and Woolf, G. (2016) Ancient Libraries. (2016) Cambridge University Press
Sauneron, S. (2000) [1988] *The Priests of Ancient* Egypt, New Edition. Translated by David Lorton. Cornell University Press
Scott, F.J. (2012) *The Oxford Handbook of Late Antiquity.* OUP USA
Siedentop, L. (2014) *Inventing the individual: The origins of Western Liberalism.*
Skinner, Q. (1978) *The foundations of modern political thought.* Vol 1. The Renaissance. Cambridge Uni Press.
Smith, P. and Findlen, P. (Eds) (2001) *Merchants and Marvels: Commerce, science and art in Early Modern Europe* Routledge
Strathern, P. (2005) *The Medici Godfathers of the Renaissance.* Pimlico edition.
Uzdavinys, A. (Editor), (2009) *The Heart of Plotinus: The Essential Enneads.* April 16, 2009. World Wisdom.
Warner, R. (1958) *Greek Philosophers.* Signet
Wilson, A.N. (2011) *The Elizabethans Farrar.* Straus and Giroux, NYC
Woolf, G. (2013) *Introduction: Approaching the ancient library* in Konig, J., Oikonomopoulou, A., Woolf, G. (Eds) (2013) Ancient Libraries. Cambridge Press

Yates, F. A. (1972) *Rosicrucian enlightenment.* Routledge & Kegan Paul

Aristotle (2009) [1995]. *Politics.* Translated by Ernest Barker and revised with introduction and notes by R. F. Stalley (1st ed.). Oxford University Press

Bacon, F. *Essays, Civil and Moral.* Vol. III, Part 1. The Harvard Classics. New York: P.F. Collier & Son, 1909–14

Locke, J. *An Essay Concerning Humane Understanding,* Volume I.

.

Chapter 1 The House of Life Pages 8 – 33

---

[i] History of Alchemy podcast https://www.podcastnik.com/history-of-alchemy-podcast

[ii] The Academy https://theboi.co.uk/the-academy

[iii] Alchemy Website http://www.alchemywebsite.com/introduction.html

[iviv] The Egyptian Knowledge of Metallurgy and Metalworking. Tehuti Research Foundation (TRF). https://egypt-tehuti.org/vibrant-ancient-egyptian-economy/egyptian-knowledge-metallurgy-metalworking/

[v] *Heliopolis* https://www.britannica.com/place/Heliopolis-ancient-city-Egypt Access 27.06.2019

[vi] Doug Metzger. *The Tower of Babel.* Episode 1. Literature and History podcast. https://literatureandhistory.com/index.php/episode-001-the-tower-of-babel

[vii] Olsen, R. (1982) *Science deified and science defied: The historical significance of science in Western Culture. University of California Press. P.37.*

[viii] Hadot, P. (1995) *Philosophy as a Way of Life: Spiritual Exercises from Socrates to Foucault.* Davidson, A. (Editor) Wiley-Blackwell.

[ix] Doug Metzger. *Before the Flood.* Episode 2. Literature and History podcast https://literatureandhistory.com/index.php/episode-002-

before-the-flood
[x] Doug Metzger. *He Who Saw the Deep: The Epic of Gilgamesh.* Episode 3. Literature and History podcast. https://literatureandhistory.com/index.php/episode-003-he-who-saw-the-deep
[xi] Russell, B. (1946) *History of Western Philosophy*. p.26-27. Routledge.
[xii] Olsen, R. (1982) *Science deified and science defied: The historical significance of science in Western Culture. University of California Press. P.47.*
[xiii] Olsen, R. (1982) *Science deified and science defied: The historical significance of science in Western Culture.* University of California Press. P.44
[xiv] Dunand, F. and Zivie-Coche, C. (2004). Gods and men in Egypt: 3000 BCE to 395 CE. Ithaca, NY: Cornell University Press. Source Wiki *Ennead* 27.07.2019. 9:54
[xv] Russell, B. (1946) *History of Western Philosophy*. p.26-27. Routledge.
[xvi] Sauneron, S. (2000) [1988]. *The Priests of Ancient Egypt*, New Edition. Translated by David Lorton. Cornell University Press. Source Wiki *Egyptian Temple* Wiki 05.05.18. 16:36
[xvii] Sauneron, S. (2000) [1988]. *The Priests of Ancient Egypt*, New Edition. Translated by David Lorton. Cornell University Press. ISBN 0-8014-8654-8. Source Wiki *Egyptian Temple* Wiki 05.05.18. 16:36
[xviii] Trainer, C. (2008) *The Merits of the Milesians* https://philosophynow.org/issues/69/The_Merits_of_the_Milesians
[xix] Doug Metzger. *The Autumn Leaves*
The Odyssey, Books 17-24. Literature and History podcast https://literatureandhistory.com/index.php/episode-14-the-autumn-leaves
[xx] Russell, B. (1946) *History of Western Philosophy*. p.31. Routledge.
[xxi] Hart, G., (2005) *The Routledge Dictionary of Egyptian Gods and Goddesses*, Routledge, second edition, Oxon, p 158 source Wikipedia *Hermes Trismegistus* 28.04.18 20:37
[xxii] Hermetic Writings. Encyclopaedia Britannica

---

https://www.britannica.com/topic/Hermetic-writings Accessed 30.06.2019

[xxiii] Lindberg, D.C. (1992). *The beginnings of Western Science: The European scientific tradition in philosophical, religious, and institutional context, prehistory to AD 1450*. University of Chicago Press 2nd edition 2007. pp.31

[xxiv] Riedweg, C. (2005) *Pythagoras: His Life, Teachings, and Influence*, Ithaca, New York: Cornell University Press, from Wikipedia Access history 05.07.2018 15:35

[xxv] Lindberg, D.C. (1992). *The beginnings of Western Science: The European scientific tradition in philosophical, religious, and institutional context, prehistory to AD 1450*. University of Chicago Press 2nd edition 2007. P.27 – 34.

[xxvi] Warner, R. (1958) *Greek Philosophers*. Signet.

[xxvii] Graham, D.W. *Heraclitus*, The Stanford Encyclopedia of Philosophy (Fall 2015 Edition), Edward N. Zalta (ed.) https://plato.stanford.edu/archives/fall2015/entries/heraclitus

[xxviii] *Heraclitus* in Wikipedia https://en.wikipedia.org/wiki/Heraclitus Version 20.06.2018 15:23

[xxix] *Heraclitus* in Wikipedia https://en.wikipedia.org/wiki/Heraclitus Version 20.06.2018 15:23

[xxx] *Parminedes* Wikipedia https://en.wikipedia.org/wiki/Parmenides Version 12.07.2018 2:30

[xxxi] Palmer, J. *Parmenides*, The Stanford Encyclopedia of Philosophy (Winter 2016 Edition), Zalta, E.N. (ed.) https://plato.stanford.edu/archives/win2016/entries/parmenides

[xxxii] DeLong, J.C. *Parmenides of Elea*. IEP. http://www.iep.utm.edu/parmenid/ Accessed 13.07.2018 18:16

[xxxiii] Russell, B. (1946/2000 Ed) History of Western Philosophy. Routledge. pp. 61

[xxxiv] *Democritus* Wikipedia https://en.wikipedia.org/wiki/Democritus Source 01.07.2018 04:18

[xxxv] *Materialism* https://www.britannica.com/topic/materialism-philosophy

[xxxvi] *Atomism* https://www.britannica.com/topic/atomism

[xxxvii] Plato c.350 BC Timaeus.

http://classics.mit.edu/Plato/timaeus.html
[xxxviii] Flegel, P. (2018) *Does Western Philosophy Have Egyptian Roots?* Philosophy Now. https://philosophynow.org/issues/128/Does_Western_Philosophy_Have_Egyptian_Roots
[xxxix] Brickhouse, T. and Smith, Nicholas D. *Plato.* Internet Encyclopedia of Philosophy (IEP) https://www.iep.utm.edu/plato/ Accessed 08.07.2018 8:00.
[xl] Brickhouse, T. and Smith, Nicholas D. *Plato.* Internet Encyclopedia of Philosophy (IEP) https://www.iep.utm.edu/plato/ Accessed 08.07.2018 8:00.
[xli] Kraut, R. (2017) *Plato.* The Stanford Encyclopedia of Philosophy (Fall 2017 Edition), Edward N. Zalta (ed.) https://plato.stanford.edu/archives/fall2017/entries/plato/
[xlii] Brickhouse, T. and Smith, Nicholas D. *Plato.* Internet Encyclopedia of Philosophy (IEP) https://www.iep.utm.edu/plato/ Accessed 08.07.2018 8:00.
[xliii] Kraut, R. (2017) *Plato.* The Stanford Encyclopedia of Philosophy (Fall 2017 Edition), Edward N. Zalta (ed.) https://plato.stanford.edu/archives/fall2017/entries/plato/
[xliv] Shields, C. *Aristotle.* (2016) The Stanford Encyclopedia of Philosophy (Winter 2016 Edition), Edward N. Zalta (ed.) https://plato.stanford.edu/archives/win2016/entries/aristotle
[xlv] Hahm, D.E. (1982). *The fifth element in Aristotle's De Philosophia: A Critical Re-Examination.* The Journal of Hellenic Studies. In *Aether* (classical element) Wikipedia (Accessed 19.1.2019) https://en.wikipedia.org/wiki/Aether_(classical_element)
[xlvi] Garvey, J. and Stangroom, J. (2012) *The Story of Philosophy: A History of Western Thought.* Quercus. pp.90
[xlvii] Aristotle (2009) *Politics.* Translated by Ernest Barker and revised with introduction and notes by Stalley, R.F. (1st ed.). Oxford University Press. pp. 320–21. Wikipedia Aristotle 13 Source 07.2018 12:34
[xlviii] Leroi, A.M. (2015). *The Lagoon: How Aristotle Invented Science.* Bloomsbury. pp.7 Wikipedia https://en.wikipedia.org/wiki/Aristotle#CITEREFLeroi2015 Source

13.07.2018 12:34
[xlix] *Aristotle* https://en.wikipedia.org/w/index.php?title=Aristotle Source 13.07.2018 12:34
[l] Ebenstein, A. and Ebenstein, W. (2002). *Introduction to Political Thinkers.* Wadsworth Group. pp. 59. From Wikipedia https://en.wikipedia.org/wiki/Aristotle Source 13.07.2018 12:34
[li] Olsen, R. (1982) *Science deified and science defied: The historical significance of science in Western Culture.* University of California Press. pp.207

Chapter 2 The City of the Mind Pages 34 - 45

[lii] Mason, I.G. *Cosmopolitanism then and now.* St. Lawrence Institute for the Advancement of Learning. http://www.stlawrenceinstitute.org/vol14mas.html
[liii] Russell, B. (1946/2000 Ed) *History of Western Philosophy.* pp. 230. Routledge
[liv] Armstrong, A.H. (1989) *An Introduction to Ancient Philosophy.* Rowman & Littlefield. pp.109
[lv] Ribeiro, G.L. (2003) *What is Cosmopolitanism*? First published in International Encyclopedia of Social and Behavioral Sciences (4): 2842-45, Elsevier, London, 2001.
[lvi] Russell, B. (1946/2000 Ed) *History of Western Philosophy.* pp. 230. Routledge
[lvii] Ryholt, K. (2016) *Libraries in ancient Egypt* p.36. Eds. König, J, Oikonomopoulou, K. and Woolf, G. (2016) *Ancient Libraries.* Cambridge University Press
[lviii] El-Abbadi, M. (modified Apr 17, 2019) *Library of Alexandria.* Enclyclopaedia Britannica https://www.britannica.com/topic/Library-of-Alexandria
[lix] Mark, J. J. (2018, May 02). Alexandria, Egypt. Ancient History Encyclopedia. Retrieved from https://www.ancient.eu/alexandria/
[lx] Mouseion www.dailywriting.net. Retrieved 2018-03-18. Source Wikipedia *Musaeum* 18.03.18. 11.59
[lxi] Mouseion www.dailywriting.net. Retrieved 2018-03-18. Source Wikipedia *Musaeum* 18.03.18. 11.59

[lxii] El-Abbadi, M. (modified Apr 17, 2019) *Library of Alexandria: Registration and classification of books.* Enclyclopaedia Britannica https://www.britannica.com/topic/Library-of-Alexandria/Other-languages#ref334081

[lxiii] Mason, M.K. *Alexandria and the Hellenistic World* http://www.moyak.com/papers/ancient-alexandria.html

[lxiv] Mason, M.K. *Alexandria and the Hellenistic World* http://www.moyak.com/papers/ancient-alexandria.html

[lxv] *The Spread of Hellenistic Culture.* Classzone.com http://www.sps186.org/downloads/basic/727164/ch5_5.pdf

[lxvi] *Ostanes.* (2002) Encyclopædia Iranica http://www.iranicaonline.org/articles/ostanes Accessed. 30.06.2019

[lxvii] Lindberg, D.C. (2010) *The Beginnings of Western Science: The European Scientific Tradition in philosophical, religious and institutional context, prehistory to A.D. 1450.* University of Chicago Press. Second edition. pp.163

[lxviii] Mark, J.M. (1st November 2018) *The Hellenistic World: The World of Alexander the Great.* https://www.ancient.eu/article/94/the-hellenistic-world-the-world-of-alexander-the-g/

[lxix] Russell, B. (1946/2000 Ed) History of Western Philosophy. P. 233. Routledge

[lxx] Mason, M.K. *Alexandria and the Hellenistic World* http://www.moyak.com/papers/ancient-alexandria.html

[lxxi] Mason, M.K. *Alexandria and the Hellenistic World* http://www.moyak.com/papers/ancient-alexandria.html

[lxxii] Russell, B. (1946/2000 Ed) History of Western Philosophy. pp. 230. Routledge

[lxxiii] Russell, B. (1946/2000 Ed) History of Western Philosophy. P. 237. Routledge

[lxxiv] Later Antiquity. The History of Philosophy Without Any Gaps https://historyofphilosophy.net/later-antiquity

[lxxv] Fieser, J. (9/1/2017) *Hellenistic Philosophy* from The History of Philosophy: A Short Survey https://www.utm.edu/staff/jfieser/class/110/3-hellenistic.htm

[lxxvi] Marcum, J.A. *The philosophy of medicine.* The internet

encyclopedia of philosophy.
https://www.iep.utm.edu/medicine/#SH2a Accessed 20.06.2018 6:09
[lxxvii] Saunders, J.L. *Stoicism.* Encyclopaedia Britannica.
https://www.britannica.com/topic/Stoicism

Chapter 3 The Temple of Liberty Pages 46 - 68

[lxxviii] Andriotis, N.P. *History of the Greek Language* Koine Greek Wikipedia 19.10.18 9:57
[lxxix]Saller, R.P. (January 11, 2019). Ancient Rome. Encyclopædia Britannica. https://www.britannica.com/place/ancient-Rome/Intellectual-life-of-the-Late-Republic. Access: June 11, 2019
[lxxx] Saller, R.P. (January 11, 2019). Ancient Rome. Encyclopædia Britannica. https://www.britannica.com/place/ancient-Rome/Intellectual-life-of-the-Late-Republic. Access: June 11, 2019
[lxxxi] Saller, R.P. (January 11, 2019). Ancient Rome. Encyclopædia Britannica. https://www.britannica.com/place/ancient-Rome/Intellectual-life-of-the-Late-Republic. Access: June 11, 2019
[lxxxii] USU 1320: History and Civilization. SECTION 8. The Fall of Rome: Facts and Fictions
http://www.usu.edu/markdamen/1320Hist&Civ/chapters/08ROMFAL.htm
[lxxxiii] Haviaras, A.A. *Gaius Asinius Pollio and the first Public Library in Ancient Rome.* 23.07.2017.
https://eaglesanddragonspublishing.com/gaius-asinius-pollio-and-the-first-public-library-in-ancient-rome/
[lxxxiv] Platner, S. Ball. (as completed and revised by Thomas Ashby): *Atrium Libertatis.* A Topographical Dictionary of Ancient Rome, London: Oxford University Press, 1929.
http://penelope.uchicago.edu/Thayer/E/Gazetteer/Places/Europe/Italy/Lazio/Roma/Rome/_Texts/PLATOP*/Atrium_Libertatis.html
[lxxxv] Jerry Fielden (2001) Private Libraries in Ancient Rome
http://www.jerryfielden.net/essays/privatelibs.htm
[lxxxvi] Kilgour, F.G. (1998) *The Evolution of the Book.* School of Library and Information Sciences Frederick G Kilgour Oxford University Press. pp.45.

[lxxxvii] Furedi, F. (2013) *Authority: A sociological history.* Cambridge University Press. pp.82.
[lxxxviii] Metzger, D. *The Uncuttables: Lucretius' On the Nature of Things and Epicurean Philosophy* Episode 45. https://literatureandhistory.com/index.php/episode-045-the-uncuttables
[lxxxix] Metzger, D. *All Is In Flux: Ovid's Metamorphoses*, Books 11-15. Episode 63. https://literatureandhistory.com/index.php/episode-063-all-is-in-flux
[xc] Siedentop, L. (2014) *Inventing the individual: The origins of Western Liberalism.* pp.52. Penguin
[xci] Siedentop, L. (2014) *Inventing the individual: The origins of Western Liberalism.* pp.53. Penguin.
[xcii] Siedentop, L. (2014) *Inventing the individual: The origins of Western Liberalism.* pp.51. Penguin.
[xciii] The School of Alexandria and the Gnostics http://www.copticchurch.net/topics/patrology/schoolofalex/I-Intro/chapter4.html
[xciv] Moore, E, *Gnosticism* https://www.iep.utm.edu/gnostic/
[xcv] The School of Alexandria and the Gnostics http://www.copticchurch.net/topics/patrology/schoolofalex/I-Intro/chapter4.html
[xcvi] Wildberg, C. (2016) *Neoplatonism.* The Stanford Encyclopedia of Philosophy (Spring 2016 Edition), Edward N. Zalta (ed.) https://plato.stanford.edu/archives/spr2016/entries/neoplatonism
[xcvii] Gerson, Lloyd, *Plotinus.* The Stanford Encyclopedia of Philosophy (Fall 2018 Edition), Edward N. Zalta (ed.) https://plato.stanford.edu/entries/plotinus/
[xcviii] Adamson, P. & Taylor, R.C. (2005) *The Cambridge Companion to Arabic Philosophy*, Cambridge University Press.
[xcix] The Basics of Philosophy. http://www.philosophybasics.com/branch_metaphysics.html
[c] Adamson, P. (07.10.2012) Ep. 97 - *A Tale of Two Cities: The Last Pagan Philosophers.* A history of philosophy without any gaps. http://historyofphilosophy.net/last-pagans
[ci] Johnston, S.I. (2005) *Divination: Greek And Roman Divination:*

Encyclopedia of Religion. Thomson Gale. https://www.encyclopedia.com/environment/encyclopedias-almanacs-transcripts-and-maps/divination-greek-and-roman-divination

[cii] Fowden 1993: pp65–68 source Wikipedia *Hermes Trismegistus* 28.04.18 20:37

[ciii] Murker, D. *Stages of Ascension in Hermetic Rebirth* Esoteric.msu.edu. http://www.esoteric.msu.edu/Merkur.html Retrieved 2015-06-25. source Wikipedia Hermes Trismegistus 28.04.18 20:37

[civ] Hermes Trismegistus http://www.crystalinks.com/hermes_trismegistus.html Accessed 24.09.18

[cv] Goodrick-Clarke, N. (2008) *The Western Esoteric Traditions: A Historical Introduction* p.20 Oxford Uni Press. From Faivre, Ancient and Medieval Sources. p. 5.

[cvi] Cobb, C. and Goldwhite, H. (2002) *Creations of Fire: Chemistry's Lively History from Alchemy to the Atomic Age.* Basic Books, pp. 36-37

[cvii] Principe, L.M. (2012) *The secrets of alchemy.* University of Chicago Press, pp. 9-14.

[cviii] Cobb, C. and Goldwhite, H. (2002) *Creations of Fire: Chemistry's Lively History from Alchemy to the Atomic Age.* Basic Books, pp. 38

[cix] Principe, L.M. (2012) *The secrets of alchemy.* University of Chicago Press, pp. 22

[cx] Russell, B. (1946) *History of Western Philosophy.* p.236. Routledge.

[cxi] Fielden, G. (2001) *Private Libraries in Ancient Rome* http://www.jerryfielden.net/essays/privatelibs.htm

[cxii] Various authors. *The Byzantine Empire.* https://www.britannica.com/topic/education/The-Byzantine-Empire

[cxiii] Lindberg, D.C. (2010) *The Beginnings of Western Science: The European Scientific Tradition in philosophical, religious and institutional context, prehistory to A.D. 1450.* University of Chicago

Press. Second edition. pp.163

[cxiv] Lindberg, D.C. (2010) *The Beginnings of Western Science: The European Scientific Tradition in philosophical, religious and institutional context, prehistory to A.D. 1450*. University of Chicago Press. Second edition. pp.164

[cxv] Lindberg, D.C. (2010) *The Beginnings of Western Science: The European Scientific Tradition in philosophical, religious and institutional context, prehistory to A.D. 1450*. University of Chicago Press. Second edition. pp.164

[cxvi] Blumenthal, H.J. (1993) *Alexandria as a Centre of Greek Philosophy in Later Classical Antiquity*. p.314 Illinois Classical Studies Vol. 18 https://www.ideals.illinois.edu/bitstream/handle/2142/12975/illinoisclassica181993BLUMENTHAL.pdf?sequence=2

[cxvii] Tornau, C. Saint Augustine. The Stanford Encyclopedia of Philosophy (Winter 2019 Edition), Edward N. Zalta (ed.) https://plato.stanford.edu/entries/augustine/

[cxviii] Hintikka, J. *Logic*. Encyclopaedia Britannica. LAST UPDATED: Apr 25, 2018 https://www.britannica.com/topic/logic

[cxix] Woolf, G. (2013) *Introduction: Approaching the ancient library* p.16 in Konig, J., Oikonomopoulou, A., Woolf, G. (Eds) (2013) *Ancient Libraries.* Cambridge Press

[cxx] Fielden, G. (2001) *Private Libraries in Ancient Rome* http://www.jerryfielden.net/essays/privatelibs.htm

Chapter 4 The House of Wisdom Pages 69 - 91

[cxxi] Fitzgerald Johnson, Scott. (2012) *The Oxford Handbook of Late Antiquity*. OUP USA, 2012 pp.302

[cxxii] Malik, K. (2014) *The Quest for a Moral Compass*. Atlantic Books. pp.122

[cxxiii] Afsaruddin, A. *Umayyad dynasty: Islamic History*. Encyclopaedia Britannica https://www.britannica.com/topic/Umayyad-dynasty-Islamic-history

[cxxiv] Burns, R. (2005) *Damascus: A History*. Psychology Press.

[cxxv] Lapidus, I.M. (2014) *A History of Islamic Societies*: Third Edition. Cambridge University Press. pp.50-52

[cxxvi] Al-Khalili, J. (2012) *The House of Wisdom: How Arabic Science Saved Ancient Knowledge and Gave Us the Renaissance.* Penguin Books

[cxxvii] Afsaruddin, A. *Umayyad dynasty: Islamic History.* Encyclopaedia Britannica https://www.britannica.com/topic/Umayyad-dynasty-Islamic-history

[cxxviii] Hoyland, R.G. (2014) *In God's Path: The Arab Conquests and the Creation of an Islamic Empire.* Oxford University Press.

[cxxix] Ferrario, G. (Fall 2007) *Al-Kimiya: Notes on Arabic Alchemy.* Science History. https://www.sciencehistory.org/distillations/magazine/al-kimiya-notes-on-arabic-alchemy

[cxxx] Hoyland, R.G. (2014) *In God's Path: The Arab Conquests and the Creation of an Islamic Empire.* Oxford University Press. pp.230

[cxxxi] Eberly, J. (2005) *Al-Kimia: The Mystical Islamic Essence of the Sacred Art of Alchemy.* Sophia Perennis.

[cxxxii] Syed Nomanul Haq. (6 Dec 2012) *Names, Natures and Things: The Alchemist Jābir ibn Hayyān and his Kitāb al-Ahjār (Book of Stones).* Springer Science & Business Media. Source Wikipedia *Jabir ibn Hayyan* 10.06.2018. 13:06.

[cxxxiii] Syed Nomanul Haq. (6 Dec 2012) *Names, Natures and Things: The Alchemist Jābir ibn Hayyān and his Kitāb al-Ahjār (Book of Stones).* Springer Science & Business Media. Source Wikipedia *Jabir ibn Hayyan* 10.06.2018. 13:06.

[cxxxiv] Ragai, Jehane (1992), *The Philosopher's Stone: Alchemy and Chemistry,* Journal of Comparative Poetics, 12 (Metaphor and Allegory in the Middle Ages): 58–77. Source Wikipedia *Philosophers Stone*

[cxxxv] *Abbasid Caliphate.* Source https://wiki2.org/en/Abbasid_Caliphate

[cxxxvi] D'Acona, C. (2005) *Chp 2. Greek into Arabic: Neoplatonism in translation.* pp.18 in Adamson, P. and Taylor, R.C. (2005) The Cambridge Companion to Arabic Philosophy. Cambridge

University Press.
[cxxxvii] *The Round City of Baghdad* http://www.amusingplanet.com/2016/07/the-round-city-of-baghdad.html
[cxxxviii] Gutas, D. (1998) *Greek Thought, Arabic Culture: The Graeco-Arabic Translation Movement in Baghdad and Early 'Abbasaid Society*, Routledge. p.52
[cxxxix] Gutas, D. (1998) *Greek Thought, Arabic Culture: The Graeco-Arabic Translation Movement in Baghdad and Early 'Abbasaid Society*, Routledge. p.60
[cxl] Hoyland, R.G. (2014) *In God's Path: The Arab Conquests and the Creation of an Islamic Empire.* Oxford University Press.
[cxli] Hoyland, R.G. (2014) *In God's Path: The Arab Conquests and the Creation of an Islamic Empire.* Oxford University Press. pp.205
[cxlii] In Our Time 28.06.2012 *Al-Kindi.* BBC Radio 4
[cxliii] *Islam's Gift of Paper to the West.* Web.utk.edu. 2001-12-29. Archived from the original on 2015-05-03. Retrieved 2014-04-11. Source Wikipedia *The Islamic Golden Age* 11.06.2018. 18:25
[cxliv] Gutas, D. (1998) *Greek Thought, Arabic Culture: The Graeco-Arabic Translation Movement in Baghdad and Early 'Abbasaid Society*, Routledge.
[cxlv] Gutas, D. (1998) *Greek Thought, Arabic Culture: The Graeco-Arabic Translation Movement in Baghdad and Early 'Abbasaid Society*, Routledge. pp.133
[cxlvi] Gutas, D. (1998) *Greek Thought, Arabic Culture: The Graeco-Arabic Translation Movement in Baghdad and Early 'Abbasaid Society*, Routledge.
[cxlvii] Gutas, D. (1998) *Greek Thought, Arabic Culture: The Graeco-Arabic Translation Movement in Baghdad and Early 'Abbasaid Society*, Routledge. pp.137
[cxlviii] D'Acona, C. (2005) *Chp 2. Greek into Arabic: Neoplatonism in translation.* pp.19 in Adamson, P. and Taylor, R.C. (2005) The Cambridge Companion to Arabic Philosophy. Cambridge University Press.
[cxlix] Gutas, D. (1998) *Greek Thought, Arabic Culture: The Graeco-Arabic Translation Movement in Baghdad and Early 'Abbasaid*

Society, Routledge, 1998 p.63

[cl] Uzdavinys, A. (Editor), (2009) *The Heart of Plotinus: The Essential Enneads.* April 16, 2009. World Wisdom. pp.37

[cli] In Our Time 28.06.2012 *Al-Kindi.* BBC Radio 4

[clii] Lyons, J. (2009), *The House of Wisdom: How the Arabs Transformed Western Civilization*, New York: Bloomsbury Press. Source Wikipedia House of wisdom 26.05.2018 21:58

[cliii] Fakhry, M. *A History of Islamic Philosophy:* Third Edition, Columbia University Press (2004), pp. 98 Source Wikipedia Muhammad ibn Zakariya al-Razi 14.06.2018 00:14

[cliv] Ferrario, G. (Fall 2007) *Al-Kimiya: Notes on Arabic Alchemy.* Science History. https://www.sciencehistory.org/distillations/magazine/al-kimiya-notes-on-arabic-alchemy

[clv]Shuttleworth, M. (Nov 23, 2010). *Islamic Alchemy.* Retrieved Jun 14, 2018 from Explorable.com: https://explorable.com/islamic-alchemy

[clvi] *Muʿtazilah.* Last updated: Apr 27, 2018 https://www.britannica.com/topic/Mutazilah

[clvii] Malik, K. (2014) *The Quest for a Moral Compass.* Atlantic Books. pp. 125

[clviii] Adamson, P. *State of Mind: al-Fārābī on Religion and Politics.* 26.05.2013. Ep.130 History of Philosophy Without Any Gaps. Kings College London. https://historyofphilosophy.net/al-farabi-political

[clix] Gutas, D. *Ibn Sina [Avicenna],* The Stanford Encyclopedia of Philosophy (Fall 2016 Edition), Edward N. Zalta (ed.) https://plato.stanford.edu/archives/fall2016/entries/ibn-sina/

[clx] Gutas, D. *The Empiricism of Avicenna.* Oriens, Volume 40, Issue 2, pages 391 – 436 Publication Year :2012. Brillonline.com

[clxi] Adamson, P. *Into Thin Air: Avicenna on the Soul.* 15.09.2013. Ep.141 History of Philosophy Without Any Gaps. Kings College London; https://en.wikipedia.org/wiki/Avicenna#Argument_for_God.27s_existence

[clxii] Malik, K. (2014) *The Quest for a Moral Compass.* Atlantic Books. pp.140

[clxiii] Adamson, P. *Miracle Worker: al-Ghazālī against the Philosophers.* 06.10.2013. Ep.144 History of Philosophy Without Any Gaps. Kings College London. https://historyofphilosophy.net/al-ghazali-incoherence

[clxiv] History of the Arabs. History World http://www.historyworld.net/wrldhis/PlainTextHistories.asp?groupid=938&HistoryID=aa94&gtrack=pthc#ixzz4sql3ROuF

[clxv] Lunde, P. *Science in Al-Andalus* Unity Productions Foundation. This article appeared on pages 20-27 of the Al-Andalus print edition of Saudi Aramco World. http://www.islamicspain.tv/Arts-and-Science/science_in_al-andalus.htm

[clxvi] From: Thomas Hockey et al. (eds.). *The Biographical Encyclopedia of Astronomers,* Springer Reference. New York: Springer, 2007, pp. 727-728 https://islamsci.mcgill.ca/RASI/BEA/Majriti_BEA.htm

[clxvii] Harris, M. (1999) *History of Libraries in the Western* World 4th ed pp.81

[clxviii] Lunde, P. *Science in Al-Andalus* Unity Productions Foundation. This article appeared on pages 20-27 of the Al-Andalus print edition of Saudi Aramco World. http://www.islamicspain.tv/Arts-and-Science/science_in_al-andalus.htm

[clxix] Malik, K. *The poetry of an old atheist.* Pandemonium. https://kenanmalik.wordpress.com/2011/04/25/old-atheist/

[clxx] Russell, B. (1946/2000 Ed) *History of Western Philosophy.* Routledge. P. 420

[clxxi] Hintikka, J. *Logic.* Encyclopaedia Britannica. LAST UPDATED: Apr 25, 2018 https://www.britannica.com/topic/logic

[clxxii] Adamson, P. (22.09.2013). *Dimitri Gutas on Avicenna* Ep.142 History of Philosophy Without Any Gaps. Kings College London; https://historyofphilosophy.net/avicenna-gutas

[clxxii] Al-khalili, J. (2010) *The House of Wisdom: How Arabic Science Saved Ancient Knowledge and Gave Us the Renaissance.* Penguin Books

Chapter 5 The General House of Studies Pages 92 - 112

[clxxiii] Cantor, N.F. (1993). *The Civilization of the Middle Ages: a completely revised and expanded edition of Medieval history, the life and death of a civilization.* HarperCollins. Source Wikipedia *Carolingian Renaissance* 13.06.2018 11:10

[clxxiv] Hamerly, D. *The Córdovan Library of Caliph al-Hakam II and the Case for Interculturalism.* Dominican University. pp.11 http://www.donhamerly.info/wp-content/uploads/2015/04/cordoba.pdf

[clxxv] Chandler, T. *Four Thousand Years of Urban Growth: An Historical Census*, Lewiston, NY: The Edwin Mellen Press, 1987.*Largest Cities Through History* by Matt T. Rosenberg; or The Etext Archives Archived 2008-02-11 at the Wayback Machine. *https://en.wikipedia.org/wiki/Caliphate_of_C%C3%B3rdoba#cite_note-Chandler-18 11.06.2018 21:37*

[clxxvi] Demographics of Paris Source Wikipedia 21.04.2018 12:23

[clxxvii] Hamerly, D. *The Córdovan Library of Caliph al-Hakam II and the Case for Interculturalism.* Dominican University. pp.11 http://www.donhamerly.info/wp-content/uploads/2015/04/cordoba.pdf

[clxxviii] Marshall, C. (1982). *William of Moerbeke: Translator of Archimedes.* Proceedings of the American Philosophical Society. 126 (5): 356–366. JSTOR 986212 Source Wikipedia *Scholasticism* 30.05.2018. 23:51

[clxxix] Hamerly, D. *The Córdovan Library of Caliph al-Hakam II and the Case for Interculturalism.* Dominican University. pp.5 http://www.donhamerly.info/wp-content/uploads/2015/04/cordoba.pdf

[clxxx] McInerny, R. *A history of Western Philosophy* 2.12 https://maritain.nd.edu/jmc/etext/hwp212.htm

[clxxxi] Russell, B. (1946/2000 Ed) *History of Western Philosophy*. P. 405 Routledge.

[clxxxii] East–West Schism Source Wikipedia 06.06.2018 6:40

[clxxxiii] *Isidore of Seville.* History of Economic Thought. http://www.hetwebsite.net/het/profiles/isidore.htm

[clxxxiv] Burnett, C. *The Coherence of the Arabic-Latin Translation*

Program in Toledo, 14(1/2), 249–288 (pp249 - 288) pp. 249–51, 270. Cambridge University Press https://is.muni.cz/el/1421/podzim2008/MED01/um/Burnett_Charles_2001.pdf

[clxxxv] Makhmudov Otabek Valijonovich, *Toledo School in the period of King Alfonso X.* International Conference on History, Sociology and Philosophy. Proceedings of the 1st International conference (January 15, 2017). East West Association for Advanced Studies and Higher Education GmbH. Vienna. 2017. 72 http://ppublishing.org/upload/iblock/f15/Layout_History_Sociology_Philosophy-1.pdf

[clxxxvi] Gutas, D. (1998) *Greek Thought, Arabic Culture: The Graeco-Arabic Translation Movement in Baghdad and Early 'Abbasaid Society*, Routledge p.181.

[clxxxvii] Russell, B. (1946/2000 Ed) *History of Western Philosophy.* P. 385. Routledge

[clxxxviii] Olsen, R. (1982) *Science deified and science defied: The historical significance of science in Western Culture.* University of California Press. P.194

[clxxxix] *Scholasticism.* The basics of philosophy http://www.philosophybasics.com/movements_scholasticism.htm

[cxc]Burnett, C. *The Coherence of the Arabic-Latin Translation Program in Toledo* 14(1/2), 249–288 (pp249 - 288) pp. 249–51, 270. Cambridge University Press https://is.muni.cz/el/1421/podzim2008/MED01/um/Burnett_Charles_2001.pdf

[cxci] Spade, P.V. *Medieval Philosophy.* The Stanford Encyclopedia of Philosophy (Summer 2018 Edition), Edward N. Zalta (ed.), forthcoming https://plato.stanford.edu/archives/sum2018/entries/medieval-philosophy/

[cxcii]Spade, P.V.. *Medieval Philosophy.* The Stanford Encyclopedia of Philosophy (Summer 2018 Edition), Edward N. Zalta (ed.), forthcoming https://plato.stanford.edu/archives/sum2018/entries/medieval-philosophy/

[cxciii] Olsen, R. (1982) *Science deified and science defied: The historical significance of science in Western Culture.* University of California Press. P.195

[cxciv] Aristotle and the University of Paris in Medieval Western Thought. Wed 02.07.2014 at 21:10:05 https://everything2.com/title/Aristotle+and+the+University+of+Paris

[cxcv] Gilson, 1955, p.402 in Skinner, Q. 1978. *The foundations of modern political thought.* Vol 1. The Renaissance. Cambridge Uni Press. P.51

[cxcvi] Aquinas, T. *Summa Theologica* http://summatheologica.info/summa/questions/?q=13&a=72

[cxcvii] Hackett, J. *Roger Bacon,* The Stanford Encyclopaedia of Philosophy (Spring 2015 Edition), Edward N. Zalta (ed.), https://plato.stanford.edu/archives/spr2015/entries/roger-bacon/

[cxcviii] Antolic-Piper, P. *Roger Bacon.* IEP https://www.iep.utm.edu/bacon-ro/#H2 (Accessed 13.08.18 8:04)

[cxcix] Antolic-Piper, P. *Roger Bacon.* IEP https://www.iep.utm.edu/bacon-ro/#H2 (Accessed 13.08.18 8:30)

[cc] *Ramon Llull.* Wikipedia 14.06.2018 13:25

[cci] Olsen, R. (1982*) Science deified and science defied: The historical significance of science in Western Culture.* University of California Press. (p.196)

[ccii] Bailey, M.D. (2008) *The Age of Magicians: Periodization in the History of European Magic.* Iowa State University.

[cciii] Bailey, Michael D. (2008) *The Age of Magicians: Periodization in the History of European Magic.* Iowa State University.

[cciv] Bailey, Michael D. (2008) *The Age of Magicians: Periodization in the History of European Magic.* Iowa State University.

[ccv] Source Wikipedia Witch trials in the early modern period – see note 12. 11.06.2018 19:40

[ccvi] Bailey, Michael D. (2008) *The Age of Magicians: Periodization in the History of European Magic.* Iowa State University.

[ccvii] Woods, Thomas. (2005) *How the Catholic Church Built Western Civilization.* p 91-92. Washington, DC: Regnery; ISBN 0-89526-038-7 Source Wikipedia Condemnations of 1210–1277 10.05.2018

21:36
[ccviii] Olsen, R. (1982) *Science deified and science defied: The historical significance of science in Western Culture.* University of California Press. P.199-203
[ccix] Olsen, R. (1982) *Science deified and science defied: The historical significance of science in Western Culture.* University of California Press. P.201-201

Chapter 6 The House of Joy Pages 113 - 130

[ccx] Art Trade 1400 – 1600 http://bluenetworks.weebly.com/art-trade-between-the-low-counties-and-italy-1400-1600.html
[ccxi] Military history of Italy. *Military history of Italy* Wikipedia
[ccxii] Skinner, Q. 1978. *The foundations of modern political thought.* Vol 1. The Renaissance. Cambridge Uni Press. P. 53
[ccxiii] Skinner, Q. 1978. *The foundations of modern political thought.* Vol 1. The Renaissance. Cambridge Uni Press. p.93
[ccxiv] Meehan, W.F. (2007). *The importance of Cosimo de Medici in library history.* Indiana libraries. Vol 26. No. 3. Source Wikipedia *Cosimo de Medici*
[ccxv] Strathern, P. (2005) *The Medici Godfathers of the Renaissance.* (p.95). Pimlico edition.
[ccxvi] Wikipedia *Cosimo de Medici*
[ccxvii] Nelles, P. *Renaissance Libraries (2001)* Stam, (ed.) International Dictionary of Library History 151. http://www.historyofinformation.com/expanded.php?id=336
[ccxviii] Strathern, P. (2005) *The Medici Godfathers of the Renaissance.* (p.95). Pimlico edition.
[ccxix] *Vittorino da Feltre* Wikipedia
[ccxx] Durant, W. (1953). *The Renaissance. The Story of Civilization.*p.250 5. New York: Simon and Schuster.
[ccxxi] *Leon Battista Alberti.*Encylopaedia Britannica
[ccxxii] *Renaissance Man.* Encylopaedia Britannica
[ccxxiii] Adamson, P. (30.06.2019). *Old News – Introduction to the Italian Renaissance. Episode* 328. The History of Philosophy without Any Gaps. Kings College London & LMU

https://historyofphilosophy.net/renaissance-introduction

[ccxxiv] Olsen, R. (1982) *Science deified and science defied: The historical significance of science in Western Culture.* University of California Press. pp.213

[ccxxv] Olsen, R. (1982) *Science deified and science defied: The historical significance of science in Western Culture.* University of California Press. pp.218-220

[ccxxvi] Salaman, C. and Van Oyen, D. and Wharton, W.D. and Mahé, J (2000). *The Way of Hermes: New Translations of The Corpus Hermeticum and The Definitions of Hermes Trismegistus to Asclepius.* Rochester: Inner Traditions. Wikipedia *Hermeticism.*

[ccxxvii] *The legendary Emerald Tablet 10.*08.2014 23:14 Ancient Origins. http://www.ancient-origins.net/myths-legends/legendary-emerald-tablet-001956

[ccxxviii] Olsen, R. (1982) *Science deified and science defied: The historical significance of science in Western Culture.* University of California Press. pp.21

[ccxxix] Olsen, R. (1982) *Science deified and science defied: The historical significance of science in Western Culture.* University of California Press. pp.232

[ccxxx] Goodrick-Clarke, N. (2008) The Western Esoteric Traditions: A Historical Introduction p.45 Oxford Uni Press

[ccxxxi] Newman. W.R. (2005) *Promethean Ambitions: Alchemy and the Quest to Perfect Nature* (p.84) Chicago University Press.

[ccxxxii] Skinner, Q. The foundations of modern political thought. Vol 1. The Renaissance. (p. 94 – 97). Cambridge University Press

[ccxxxiii] Skinner, Q. The foundations of modern political thought. Vol 1. The Renaissance. (p.145). Cambridge University Press

[ccxxxiv] Robin, D. *Publishing Women: Salons, The Presses, and the counter-reformation in sixteenth-century Italy.* University Chicago Press.

Chapter 7 The Cabinet of Curiosities Pages 131 - 164

[ccxxxv] Hobson, A. (1979) *Great Libraries.* D.H. Greaves Ltd.

[ccxxxvi] Hobson, A. (1979) *Great Libraries.* D.H. Greaves Ltd p.12

[ccxxxvii] Olsen, R. (1982) *Science deified and science defied: The historical significance of science in Western Culture.* University of California Press. P.255

[ccxxxviii] Baker-Smith, D. *Thomas More, The Stanford Encyclopaedia of Philosophy* (Spring 2014 Edition), Edward N. Zalta (ed.) https://plato.stanford.edu/archives/spr2014/entries/thomas-more/

[ccxxxix] Rummel, Erika, *Desiderius Erasmus* The Stanford Encyclopedia of Philosophy (Winter 2017 Edition), Edward N. Zalta (ed.) https://plato.stanford.edu/archives/win2017/entries/erasmus/

[ccxl] Rummel, Erika, *Desiderius Erasmus* The Stanford Encyclopedia of Philosophy (Winter 2017 Edition), Edward N. Zalta (ed.) https://plato.stanford.edu/archives/win2017/entries/erasmus/

[ccxli] Hill, G. (Jul 8, 2016) *Augustine's influence on Calvin, Luther and Zwingli.* https://theglobalchurchproject.com/augustines-influence-calvin-luther-zwingli/ Church, Theology. Accessed 19.06.2018 18:43

[ccxlii] See Note 8 Source Wikipedia Nicolaus Copernicus Source 15.06.2018 15:36

[ccxliii] Olsen, R. (1982) *Science deified and science defied: The historical significance of science in Western Culture.* University of California Press. P.252-254

[ccxliv] Eggen, O.J. (11.05.2017) *Tycho Brahe.* https://www.britannica.com/biography/Tycho-Brahe-Danish-astronomer

[ccxlv] Tycho Brahe (1546-1601). *The Galileo Project.* Accessed 19.06.2016 18:49. http://galileo.rice.edu/sci/brahe.html

[ccxlvi] D. Knox. *Giordano Bruno.* The Stanford Encyclopedia of Philosophy (Summer 2019 Edition), Edward N. Zalta (ed.). https://plato.stanford.edu/archives/sum2019/entries/bruno

[ccxlvii] Stanford Encyclopaedia of Philosophy: *Natural Philosophy in the Renaissance.* First published Tue Apr 14, 2015; substantive revision Tue Aug 30, 2016 https://plato.stanford.edu/entries/natphil-ren/#OldCosNewCos

[ccxlviii] Hatfield, G. *René Descartes.* The Stanford Encyclopedia of Philosophy (Summer 2018 Edition), Edward N. Zalta (ed.). https://plato.stanford.edu/archives/sum2018/entries/descartes

---

[ccxlix] Russell, B. (1946/2000 Ed) History of Western Philosophy. Routledge. pp. 517 – 523

[ccl] Goodrick-Clarke, N. (2008) *The Western Esoteric Traditions: A Historical Introduction* p.60 Oxford Uni Press. Nauert, Agrippa and the Crisis of Renaissance Thought, pp. 35–54.

[ccli] Goodrick-Clarke, N. (2008) *The Western Esoteric Traditions: A Historical Introduction* p.49 Oxford Uni Press

[cclii] Goodrick-Clarke, N. (2008) *The Western Esoteric Traditions: A Historical Introduction* p.71 Oxford Uni Press

[ccliii] Goodrick-Clarke, N. (2008) *The Western Esoteric Traditions: A Historical Introduction* p.59 Oxford Uni Press

[ccliv] Butler, E.M. (1952) *The fortunes of Faust* (p.ix) Cambridge University Press

[cclv]Nummedal, T. (2013) *Alchemy and Religion in Christian Europe* (p.311) AMBIX

[cclvi] Goodrick-Clarke, N. (2008) *The Western Esoteric Traditions: A Historical Introduction* p.60 Oxford Uni Press Nauert, Agrippa and the Crisis of Renaissance Thought, pp. 35–54.

[cclvii] Source wikipedia *Trier Witch Trials* Source 08.06.2018 9:25

[cclviii]Butler, E.M. (1952) *The fortunes of Faust.* (p.4) Cambridge University Press

[cclix]Butler, E.M. (1952) *The fortunes of Faust.* (p.4) Cambridge University Press

[cclx] Goodrick-Clarke, N. (2008) *The Western Esoteric Traditions: A Historical Introduction* p.60 Oxford Uni Press Nauert, Agrippa and the Crisis of Renaissance Thought, pp. 35–54.

[cclxi] Janacek, B. (2011) *Alchemical Belief Occultism in the Religious Culture of Early Modern England* Penn State Press. p.3

[cclxii] Goodrick-Clarke, N. (2008) *The Western Esoteric Traditions: A Historical Introduction* p.60 Oxford Uni Press. Nauert, Agrippa and the Crisis of Renaissance Thought, pp. 35–54.

[cclxiii] Hargrave, J.G. (01.05.2013) *Paracelsus.* https://www.britannica.com/biography/Paracelsus#ref5505

[cclxiv] Schaber, J. (1993). *Paracelsus*, lat. Pseudonym von {Philippus Aureolus} Theophrastus Bombastus von Hohenheim. In Bautz, Traugott.Biographisch-Bibliographisches Kirchenlexikon (BBKL)

(in German).6. Herzberg: Bautz. cols. 1502–1528.ISBN3-88309-044-1. Source Wikipedia *Paracelsus* 23.05.20 8:52

cclxv Hargrave, J.G. (01.05.2013) *Paracelsus.* Encyclopaedia Britannica.
https://www.britannica.com/biography/Paracelsus#ref5505

cclxvi Hargrave, J.G. (26.02.2019) Paracelsus. Encyclopædia Britannica. https://www.britannica.com/biography/Paracelsus. Accessed 28.07.2019

cclxvii Cockran, A. *Paracelsus: Alchemical Genius of the Middle Ages.* The Alchemy Lab. Accessed 19.06.2018 18:54
https://www.alchemylab.com/paracelsus.htm#The%20Hermetic%20Heretic

cclxviii *Paracelsus.* The Science Museum. Accessed 19.06.2018 18:59
http://broughttolife.sciencemuseum.org.uk/broughttolife/people/paracelsus

cclxix Goodrick-Clarke, N. (2008*) The Western Esoteric Traditions: A Historical Introduction* p.75 Oxford Uni Press

cclxx Goodrick-Clarke, N. (2008) *The Western Esoteric Traditions: A Historical Introduction* p.74 Oxford Uni Press

cclxxi Hargrave, J.G. (01.05.2013) *Paracelsus.* Encyclopaedia Britannica.
https://www.britannica.com/biography/Paracelsus#ref5505

cclxxii Goodrick-Clarke, N. (2008) *The Western Esoteric Traditions: A Historical Introduction* p.79 Oxford Uni Press

cclxxiii Hargrave, John, G. (26.02.2019) *Paracelsus.* Encyclopædia Britannica. https://www.britannica.com/biography/Paracelsus. Accessed 28.07.2019

cclxxiv Hargrave, John, G. (26.02.2019) *Paracelsus.* Encyclopædia Britannica. https://www.britannica.com/biography/Paracelsus. Accessed 28.07.2019

cclxxv *Alexander von Suchten.* Complete Dictionary of Scientific Biography. *Encyclopedia.com.* 19 Jun. 2018
https://www.encyclopedia.com/science/dictionaries-thesauruses-pictures-and-press-releases/suchten-alexander-von

cclxxvi Olsen, R. (1982) *Science deified and science defied: The historical significance of science in Western Culture.* University of

California Press. P.208

[cclxxvii] Nummedal, T.E. (2002) *Practical alchemy and commercial exchange in the Holy Roman Empire.* p.215. in Pamela Smith, Paula Findlen (ed) (2002) *Merchants and Marvels: Commerce, Science, and Art in Early Modern Europe.* Routledge.

[cclxxviii] Olsen, R. (1982) *Science deified and science defied: The historical significance of science in Western Culture.* University of California Press. P.226

[cclxxix] Goodrick-Clarke, N. (2008) *The Western Esoteric Traditions: A Historical Introduction* p.62 Oxford Uni Press

[cclxxx] Nummedal, T.E. (2002) *Practical alchemy and commercial exchange in the Holy Roman Empire.* p.215. in Pamela Smith, Paula Findlen (ed) (2002) *Merchants and Marvels: Commerce, Science, and Art in Early Modern Europe.* Routledge

[cclxxxi] Schleiner, L. (2004) *Kelly, Sir Edward (1555–1597/8),* Oxford Dictionary of National Biography, Oxford University Press, accessed 4 March 2012 Source Wikipedia *Edward Kelley*

[cclxxxii] Wilson, A.N. (2011) *The Elizabethans* Farrar. Straus and Giroux, NYC, NY. 03.06.2018 0:27

[cclxxxiii] Urszula Szulakowska. *Robert Fludd and His Images of The Divine.* The public domain reviews. Accessed 19.06.2018. 19:20. https://publicdomainreview.org/2011/09/13/robert-fludd-and-his-images-of-the-divine/

[cclxxxiv] https://en.wikipedia.org/wiki/Basil_Valentine Source 27.03.2018 18:47

[cclxxxv] Nummedal, T. (2013) *Alchemy and Religion in Christian Europe* (p.321) AMBIX

[cclxxxvi] See Kors and Peters (2000) p. 177; Accessed Wiki *Summis desiderantes affectibus* 29.07.2019

[cclxxxvii] Nummedal, T. (2013) *Alchemy and Religion in Christian Europe* pp.209 AMBIX

[cclxxxviii] *Accounts of the Lord High Treasurer of Scotland,* vol. iii, (1901), 99, 202, 206, 209, 330, 340, 341, 353, 355, 365, 379, 382, 389, 409. Source Wikipedia *Alchemy* Accessed 18.06.2018 19:10

[cclxxxix] Nummedal. T.E. (2007) *Alchemy and authority in the Holy Roman Empire.* The University of Chicago Press. p.85-98. Source

---

Wikipedia *Alchemy* Source 18.06.2018 19:10
[ccxc] Nummedal, T.E. (2007) *Alchemy and authority in the Holy Roman Empire.* The University of Chicago Press p.4
[ccxci] Nummedal, T.E. (2002) *Practical alchemy and commercial exchange in the Holy Roman Empire.* p.209. in Pamela Smith, Paula Findlen (ed) (2002) *Merchants and Marvels: Commerce, Science, and Art in Early Modern Europe.* Routledge
[ccxcii] Eschner, K. (AUGUST 18) 2017 *England's Witchtrials were lawful* Accessed 19.11.2019. https://www.smithsonianmag.com/smart-news/englands-witch-trials-were-lawful-180964514/.
[ccxciii] Ridgway, C. *The Elizabeth Files* http://www.elizabethfiles.com/info/tudor-life/witchcraft/ accessed 19.06.2018 16:03
[ccxciv] Eschner, K. (AUGUST 18, 2017) *England's Witchtrials were lawful* Accessed 19.11.2019. https://www.smithsonianmag.com/smart-news/englands-witch-trials-were-lawful-180964514/.
[ccxcv] Smith, P. and Findlen, P. (Eds) (2001) Merchants and Marvels: Commerce, science and art in Early Modern Europe. Routledge. p. 4 - 5
[ccxcvi] See Wikipedia *Cabinet of Curiosities* note 3
[ccxcvii] DaCosta Kaufmann, T. (197) *Remarks on the Collections of Rudolf II: The Kunstkammer as a Form of Representation.* Art Journal 38.1 (Autumn 1978:22–28). See Wikipedia *Cabinet of Curiosities.* Source 31.05.2018 21:14

Chapter 8 The New Atlantis Pages 165 – 201

[ccxcviii] Wikipedia *Thirty Years War*
[ccxcix] Izenour, GC, Bay, H.; Barker, C. *Developments of The Renaissance.* Encyclopaedia Britannica. https://www.britannica.com/art/theater-building/Developments-of-the-Renaissance
[ccc] Mullan, J. (15 Mar 2016) *Shakespeare and Italy..* British Library Discovering Literature: Shakespeare and Renaissance writers.

Creative Commons.
https://www.bl.uk/shakespeare/articles/shakespeare-and-italy

[ccci] Borman, T. (2016) *Shakespeare's Macbeth and King James's witch hunts*. This article was first published by History Extra. https://www.historyextra.com/period/elizabethan/shakespeares-macbeth-and-king-jamess-witch-hunts/

[cccii] *This great stage of fools.* https://stageoffoolsdotcom.wordpress.com/the-play/production-history/

[ccciii] Borman, T. (2016) *Shakespeare's Macbeth and King James's witch hunts*. This article was first published by History Extra. https://www.historyextra.com/period/elizabethan/shakespeares-macbeth-and-king-jamess-witch-hunts/

[ccciv] Wikipedia *Three witches*

[cccv] Trueman, C. N. (17 Mar 2015). *James I And Witchcraft*. The History Learning Site. Accessed 20 Jun 2018. https://www.historylearningsite.co.uk/stuart-england/james-i-and-witchcraft/

[cccvi] Royal Shakespeare Company. *Stage history: The history of The Tempest in performance, from 1611 when it was first performed to today.* https://www.rsc.org.uk/the-tempest/about-the-play/stage-history

[cccvii] Bryson, M. *Alchemy, Witchcraft, and the Magus Figure in The Tempest.* http://michaelbryson.net/academic/tempest.html

[cccviii] Bryson, M. *Alchemy, Witchcraft, and the Magus Figure in The Tempest.* http://michaelbryson.net/academic/tempest.html

[cccix] Reginald Scot, *Discoverie of Witchcraft* (1584) p 2. Source Wikipedia *Reginald Scot* 05.04.2018 8:58

[cccx] Carpi,D; Leiboff, M; de Gruyter, W. (2016) *Fables of the Law: Fairy Tales in a Legal Context*. GmbH & Co KG, 24 Oct 2016 p. 98 - 101

[cccxi] Trueman, C.N. (17 Mar 2015) *James I And Witchcraft*. The History Learning Site, 20 Jun 2018. https://www.historylearningsite.co.uk/stuart-england/james-i-and-witchcraft/

Chapter Notes

[cccxii] Hay, S. (2011*) The Historical Significance of Matthew Hopkins: England's Witchfinder General.*
https://www.luthercollege.edu/university/academics/impetus/spring-2011/the-historical-significance-of-matthew-hopkins-englands-witchfinder-general/

[cccxiii] Thomas, K, (1971) *Religion and the Decline of Magic*, by. 716 pp. New York, Charles Scribner's Sons, by Philip J. Greven, Jr. First Published January 1, 1972. Theology today P. 207 – 208
http://journals.sagepub.com/doi/pdf/10.1177/004057367202800415

[cccxiv] Yates, F.A. (1972) *Rosicrucian enlightenment.* Routledge & Kegan Paul
https://ia802603.us.archive.org/14/items/TheRosicrucianEnlightenment/The%20Rosicrucian%20Enlightenment.pdf

[cccxv] Birch, D.and Hooper, K. (Ed) 30 May 2013. *The Concise Oxford Companion to English Literature.* OUP Oxford.

[cccxvi] Matuk, C. (2006) *Seeing the Body: The Divergence of Ancient Chinese and Western Medical Illustration*, Journal of Biocommunication, Vol. 32, No. 1, 2006, Source Wikipedia *Empiricism* Source 27.05.2018 15:34

[cccxvii] Wikipedia *Empiricism* Accessed 05.09.2019

[cccxviii] Wikipedia *Four Causes*

[cccxix] Hatfield, G. *René Descartes.* The Stanford Encyclopedia of Philosophy (Summer 2018 Edition), Edward N. Zalta (ed.).
https://plato.stanford.edu/archives/sum2018/entries/descartes

[cccxx] Barzun, J. (2000). *From Dawn to Decadence: 500 Years of Western Cultural Life.* Harper Collins. pp.193.

[cccxxi] Wikipedia *Rene Descartes*

[cccxxii] Encyclopaedia eds. Copernican system: Astronomy,
https://www.britannica.com/science/Copernican-system

[cccxxiii] Field, J.V. *The origins of proof II: Kepler's proofs.* Plus magazine. Submitted May 1, 1999.
https://plus.maths.org/content/origins-proof-ii-keplers-proofs

[cccxxiv] Cox, L. *Who Invented the Telescope*? SPACE.com December 20, 2017 10:30pm
https://www.space.com/21950-who-invented-the-telescope.html

[cccxxv] Wikipedia *Newtons laws of universal gravitation.*

[cccxxvi] Barzun, J. (2000). From Dawn to Decadence: 500 Years of Western Cultural Life. Harper Collins. pp.193.
[cccxxvii] Levenson. T. (2009) *Newton and the counterfeiter.* Faber & Faber. pp.81
[cccxxviii] Levenson. T. (2009) *Newton and the counterfeiter.* Faber & Faber. p.81
[cccxxix] The Royal Society, August 2004 retrieved online: 2009-05-14 source JOC/EFR:
http://www-history.mcs.st-and.ac.uk/Societies/RS.html Wikipedia Royal Society.
[cccxxx] The Royal Society, August 2004 retrieved online: 2009-05-14 source JOC/EFR:
http://www-history.mcs.st-and.ac.uk/Societies/RS.html Wikipedia Royal Society.
[cccxxxi] Lisa Jardine, The Curious Life of Robert Hooke (2003), p. 88. Source Wikipedia *Hartlib Circle.*
[cccxxxii] Wikipedia *Johannes Valentinus Andreae*
[cccxxxiii] McKnight, S.A. (2005) *Francis Bacon's God.* The New Atlantis, Number 10, Fall 2005, pp. 73-100.
https://www.thenewatlantis.com/publications/francis-bacons-god
[cccxxxiv] Wikipedia *Sendivogius*
[cccxxxv] Wikipedia *Johann Rudolp Glauber*
[cccxxxvi] Wikipedia *George Starkey*
[cccxxxvii] Hildyard, R. (1999) *European Ceramics.* London: V&A Publications, p.46. Source Wikipedia *Johann Bottgar*
[cccxxxviii] Wikipedia *Cornelis Drebbel*
[cccxxxix] Levenson. T. (2009) *Newton and the counterfeiter.* Faber & Faber. pp.77 - 80
[cccxl] Mann, A. (2014) *The Strange, Secret History of Isaac Newton's Papers*. By Dry, S. Wired. 05.14.14 06:30 AM. Accessed 05.09.2019.
[cccxli] Levenson. T. (2009) *Newton and the counterfeiter.* Faber & Faber. P. 85
[cccxlii] Hobson, A. (1970) *Great libraries.* D.H. Greaves Ltd.
[cccxliii] *Dissolution of the Monasteries.* Source Wikipedia Accessed 21:29, 18 June 2019
[cccxliv] Hobson, A. (1970) *Great Libraries.* D.H. Greaves Ltd. p.174

cccxlv Hobson, A. (1970) *Great Libraries.* D.H. Greaves Ltd.
cccxlvi Hobson, A. (1970) *Great Libraries.* D.H. Greaves Ltd. p.211
cccxlvii Hobson, A. (1970) *Great Libraries.* D.H. Greaves Ltd. p.214
cccxlviii Ladborough, R.W. (1967) *The Library of Samuel Pepys.* Published in History Today Volume 17 Issue 7 July 1967. https://www.historytoday.com/rw-ladborough/library-samuel-pepys
cccxlix Kusukawa, S. (1996). *Bacon's classification of knowledge.* In M. Peltonen (Ed.), *The Cambridge Companion to Bacon* (Cambridge Companions to Philosophy, pp. 47-74). Cambridge University Press.
cccl Uzgalis, William, (2018) *John Locke.* The Stanford Encyclopedia of Philosophy (Summer 2018 Edition), Edward N. Zalta (ed.) https://plato.stanford.edu/archives/sum2018/entries/locke
cccli Wikipedia *Encyclopedia Renaissance*
ccclii John Amos Comenius. Encyclopedia of World Biography, 2nd ed. 17 Vols. Gale Research, 1998. Reproduced in Biography Resource Center. Retrieved 2 January 2010. Source Wikipedia *John Amos Comenius*
cccliii Johann Comenius (1592–1670) - Contributions, Works. http://education.stateuniversity.com/pages/1868/Comenius-Johann-1592-1670.html
cccliv Wikipedia *Hartlib Circle*
ccclv Wikipedia *John Amos Comenius*
ccclvi Gilman, D. C.; Peck, H. T.; Colby, F. M., eds. (1905). Comenius, Johann Amos. New International Encyclopedia (1st ed.). New York: Dodd, Mead. Source Wikipedia *John Amos Comenius*
ccclvii Marshall, C. (22nd May 2014). *The First Children's Picture Book, 1658's Orbis Sensualium Pictus.* Open Culture. Accessed 03.08.2019
ccclviii Paul Heidebrecht. Learning from Nature. Christian History originally published this article in Christian History Issue #13 in 1987. https://christianhistoryinstitute.org/magazine/article/learning-from-nature
ccclix Evans, G.R. (2010) *The University of Oxford: A New History.* I B Tauris & Co Ltd; 1st edn edition.

[ccclx] Thomas, D. and Chesworth, John A. Eds. (2016) *Christian-Muslim Relations. A Bibliographical History Volume 8. Northern and Eastern Europe (1600-1700).* The History of Christian-Muslim Relations, Volume: 29

[ccclxi] Evans, G.R. (2010) *The University of Oxford: A New History.* I B Tauris & Co Ltd; 1st edition.

[ccclxii] Crichton-Miller, E. (MARCH) 18, 2016 *The Grand Tour: Culture by the crateload.* FT. ttps://www.ft.com/content/1b66ef1e-eac1-11e5-bb79-2303682345c8

[ccclxiii] Buzard, J. (2002). *The Grand Tour and after (1660-1840).* In P. Hulme & T. Youngs (Eds.), The Cambridge Companion to Travel Writing (Cambridge Companions to Literature, pp. 37-52). Cambridge: Cambridge University Press. https://www.cambridge.org/core/books/cambridge-companion-to-travel-writing/grand-tour-and-after-16601840/7DB3D61309C6B631721B6296F6DF0AA9

[ccclxiv] Locke, J. *An Essay Concerning Humane Understanding,* Volume I. The Project Gutenberg EBook http://www.gutenberg.org/files/10615/10615-h/10615-h.htm

[ccclxv] Russell, G. A. (1994), *The 'Arabick' Interest of the Natural Philosophers in Seventeenth-Century England,* pp. 224–239, Brill Publishers Source Wikipedia *Ibn Tufail*

[ccclxvi] Uzgalis, W., *John Locke,* The Stanford Encyclopedia of Philosophy (Summer 2018 Edition), Edward N. Zalta (ed.) https://plato.stanford.edu/archives/sum2018/entries/locke/

[ccclxvii] *Francis Bacon: Philosopher of science.* Christianity Today. https://www.christianitytoday.com/history/people/scholarsandscientists/francis-bacon.html Source Wikipedia *Francis Bacon* 19.06.2018 22:41

[ccclxviii] Bacon, Francis. *Essays, Civil and Moral.* Vol. III, Part 1. The Harvard Classics. New York: P.F. Collier & Son, 1909–14; Bartleby.com, 2001. https://www.bartleby.com/br/00301.html

[ccclxix] Wikipedia *Robert Boyle*

[ccclxx] Brewster, David, Sir (1855) *Memoirs of the life, writings, and discoveries of Sir Isaac Newton.* Publisher Edinburgh, T. Constable and Co. Collection Americana.

Book from the collections of University of Michigan. P. P. 374-375 https://archive.org/details/memoirslifewrit02brewgoog

[ccclxxi] Schaffer, S. (1983) *Isaac Newton: His life and work.* Imperial College. https://www.youtube.com/watch?v=GvW_Y9sw6hk

[cccl xxii] Levenson. T. (2009) *Newton and the counterfeiter.* Faber & Faber. p.92

[cccl xxiii] *An Astronomical Description of the Late Comet or Blazing Star*; As it appeared in New-England in the 9th, 10th, 11th, and in the beginning of the 12th Moneth, 1664. Together with a Brief Theological Application thereof. (1665) An Online Electronic Text Edition. Samuel Danforth. Paul Royster (editor), University of Nebraska-Lincoln.https://digitalcommons.unl.edu/libraryscience/37/

[cccl xxiv]https://digitalcommons.unl.edu/cgi/viewcontent.cgi?article=1037&context=libraryscience

Reflections and Conclusions Pages 202 - 205

[i] Arendt, H. (1981) *The life of the Mind.* Vols 1 & 2. Harvest/HBJ Bookpp.62

[ii] Arendt, H. (1981) *The life of the Mind.* Vols 1 & 2. Harvest/HBJ Bookpp.62

[iii] Mary Wollstonecraft (Godwin) Shelley. *Frankenstein or The Modern Prometheus.* The Gutenberg Project.

Printed in Poland
by Amazon Fulfillment
Poland Sp. z o.o., Wrocław

53931301R00143